Crush it From the Start
50 Tips for New Teachers

#50TeacherTipsBook

Matthew Rhoads, Ed.D

Samantha Fecich, Ph.D.

Casey Jakubowski, Ph.D.

Kevin Leichtman, Ph.D.

ISBN: 978-1-7378643-4-9

DEDICATION

We dedicate this book to all new teachers. You are change makers.

TABLE OF CONTENTS

ACKNOWLEDGMENTS

Thank you to Dr. Wallace Ting and SchoolRubric for believing in this project. Thank you to our mentor teachers who helped craft us as educators. Thank you to teachers who continue to not only inspire us, but also inspire fellow teachers and students.

We would like to thank the following individuals who have assisted us in the editorial and development process. Thank you for your feedback, ideas, and perspective to help refine and guide our writing.

Dr. Lupe Buell
Nikki Torchon
Dr. Hugo Sierra
Criselda Garcia
Dr. Heather Michele
Susan Jachymiak
Richard Siegel

INTRODUCTION

Welcome to the book we wished we had when we were in your shoes. We have all thought long and hard about what we wanted to know as novice teachers. We wrote our book to be easily digestible, so there are no lengthy essays or impractical jargon. Our main goal was to have the tips to use quickly and efficiently the next day. Deep learning professional development is not something you should scrounge for. Instead, we should break it up into small bites. It's designed to be torn apart, highlighted, circled, and flagged with post-its so you can return to the ideas later on as you gain more space and focus during the year.

We are hoping you will return to this book again and again – we hope it inspires, reassures, and reaffirms what you already know. Teachers have a tough job. Research indicates that if support and guidance are not given to you as you begin your career, half of you will leave within five years. We all have hands-on classroom experience and are teacher educators. We want you to have a mentor whom we may not have had. The book is genuine. We do not hold back. We want you to know that each teaching assignment is creative, challenging, and a test of your personality, beliefs, and ability to work with learners.

We also wanted to model collaboration. Teaching used to be a one-person show back in the 19th century. A rugged sole teacher taught every grade in a one-room schoolhouse on the frontier. Today, thanks to social media and large suburban, urban, and rural schools, people are within reach - an email, a tweet, an Instagram, or a Facebook status. All of you know more than we do that technology is constantly evolving and changing the nature of education, teaching, and learning. We are all connected and can learn from each other to take on the challenges in our classrooms and schools.

Collaboration and asking for help are essential. As educators, we aim to ensure you are ready to face tomorrow and the day after. You are the author of your journey, and we want you to know how proud we are of you. Let's make a difference together.

Our "Why"

Our "Why" as educators is to support teachers and students in their learning. We want to leave this profession better than when we started. We have all experienced as teachers many good aspects of education and teaching. However, we have also had experiences that were challenging. Sometimes, we learn the hard way, and it causes us hardship. Teaching is not for the faint-hearted. Yet, we know it can improve teachers, students, and our communities. Therefore, our goal is to put our "Why" to work and support ALL teachers worldwide. Whether you teach pre-school, elementary, middle school, high school, adult education, or higher education, our "Why" is to support you and help you thrive in your context in education.

What Our Authors Want You to Know

Matt is here to inspire and lead you on this journey. Kevin will provide you with solid advice, delivered in an outstanding style. Sam has so much experience, knows the ropes, and gives you a solid path to travel. Casey provides you with actionable tips that you can put into practice right away. All four of us are here for you. We want you to know that as you read, feel free to write us notes in the margin. We won't answer unless you email. However, the four of us are super excited you are on a teaching journey and have chosen to share with us your adventure. Now, let's jump into our backgrounds briefly so you can get to know us better before your journey begins.

Let's Meet the Authors

Before we get too far, let's meet the four authors. Each author brings their own set of experiences and expertise, which we then devised into the fifty tips. Beyond reading our tips and Critical Conversations throughout the book, we hope to meet you through our professional learning network and meet you someday.

Matthew Rhoads, Ed.D. is an expert and innovator in educational technology and instructional strategy integration within online, blended, and traditional in-person classroom settings. As a practicing educator in K-12, Adult Education, and higher education, he develops EdTech tool integrations with instructional strategies to drive instruction. His experience in the classroom is teaching math, English, and social studies at the secondary level within co-taught general education and Special Education class settings. He now works coaching adult education teachers, K-12 teachers, student teachers, doctoral students, and professors and teaches tech integration courses, courses on instruction, and professional development. He also is the author of four books all on instruction and EdTech integration to amplify student learning within any classroom setting. For more about Dr. Rhoads, learn more at www.matthewrhoads.com. You can follow him on Twitter @mattrhoads1990.

Kevin Leichtman, Ph.D., has taught from seventh grade to twelfth grade as well as college undergraduates. He was an English and Language Arts and Reading teacher for eight years in South Florida and an adjunct professor at Florida Atlantic University. Kevin has authored two other books and several publications on burnout, social-emotional learning, mindset, and critical literacy. You can reach him on social media at @kevinleichtman or on his website, www.tlceducate.com.

Casey Thomas Jakubowski, Ph.D., is an expert in rural education, teacher mentoring, social studies, school improvement, and teacher leadership. Casey has 20+ years of experience teaching social studies, creating high-quality and engaging curricula, and state-level improvement processes. As an educator, Casey has written over a dozen articles on actionable lessons and has three books on teaching. Casey has led and taught all grade levels K-12, served as District leader, and is now working with doctoral students. You can find Casey on Twitter: @caseyj_edu.

Samantha (Sam) Fecich Ph.D. earned her Ph.D. in learning, design, and technology from Penn State University. In addition, she has an M.Ed. in special education and one in instructional technology, both from Penn State. Her PA certifications include K-12 special education, K-12 elementary education, and Pre-K to sixth-grade teaching. Dr. Fecich has taught education for eight years at a small liberal arts college in Pennsylvania. She is the author of "EduMagic: A Guide for Preservice Teachers" and "EduMagic Shine On A Guide for New Teachers." Dr. Fecich also hosts the EduMagic Podcast for future teachers. She is a fan of pumpkin spice lattes and hanging out with her family. You can find her on Twitter and Instagram @SFecich. Check out her work at www.SFecich.com.

Now, since you've had an opportunity to learn more about us and what we do in education, we will focus on how to navigate this book to best meet your needs as a teacher and educator.

Navigating this Book

There are several ways you can utilize this book to help you build your teaching toolkit to thrive in a sustainably and practical manner in your teaching career. Our goal is to provide multiple ways to take the content discussed in this book so you can take it and apply it to your classroom. Since it is a book of 50 tips and strategies, we will first outline how you can quickly go through the table of contents to read a tip and strategy that best fits your needs and schedule. Second, we will discuss how you can read this book chronologically before starting and moving throughout the school year.

How to Use This Book

As you can see below, the four sections are organized based on a quarter of the school year, beginning with the summer leading into a new school year. Each tip provided has been sequenced throughout the calendar year to meet the needs of teachers. However, as discussed further, we will want you to review the book's table of contents to select tips, strategies, and Critical Conversations based on what you are currently experiencing in your practice.

Section 1: The Anticipation and First Interaction

- July
- August
- September

Section 2: When the Going Gets Tough

- October
- November
- December

Section 3: The Tough Get Going

- January
- February
- March

Section 4: Are We There Yet?

- April
- May
- June

Besides the 50 tips and strategies, we also have Critical Conversations. We will outline these four conversations as opportunities to dive deep into difficult conversations and situations teachers in our profession now have to navigate. You will find Critical Conversations at the end of each four sections in this book.

Altogether, our goal is to provide an opportunity for teachers to take what we discuss and apply it to our classrooms and schools. We want to help you in your teaching journey. We will further that conversation by outlining how to take advantage of the various ways you can read this book to amplify your practice.

Using the Table of Contents. This book has four sections representing the four quarters of every school year, as illustrated in the Table of Contents. Within the four sections, we have three months of the year, starting with July. We aim to bring you tips and strategies that align with parts of the school year. For example, in section one, you will find the months July, August, and September. Our tips and strategies will focus on preparing for the school year and navigating the first few months of the year. Therefore, there are several ways to navigate and read this book, such as reading tips and strategies that best meet where you are at a given moment or as you move throughout the school year. Each format provides you, the reader, with many opportunities to read and digest the content to put into practice.

Moving through the School Year. As new teachers, there are many things on our plates. As soon as your contract is signed, many questions begin to spiral in our minds. Some of those questions might be framed around the following areas:

- Logistics as to what will be in your classroom
- Begin developing content and harnessing the curriculum
- Developing routines for your students
- Your workflow

3

- Navigating a new environment of students and colleagues
- Evaluating how you create routines
- Self-care opportunities to do these various tasks.

Ultimately, it's quite a lot to consider. Therefore, we've organized this book to help you build various skills that we feel will help you the most during a specific time of the school year. For example, one of our first tips and strategies relates to 'thinking less is more' and forming to-do lists.

Additionally, we outline several formative assessment 'Bell Ringer' strategies that will be foundational to your classroom instruction regardless of the grade and content you will be teaching. Further along in the year, we have several tips and strategies that will help invigorate and inspire you and help you navigate challenges such as burnout, a school strategy, and self-advocating for yourself to obtain support. As you can see, the goal is strategically placing these tips and strategies throughout the year for you.

Regular Entries vs. Critical Conversations. Our goal is to provide tips and strategies that can quickly be read and applied to your classroom and practice. The 50 regular entries represent the 50 tips and strategies built to do this. Yet, we felt several topics that required an in-depth conversation in the form of a Critical Conversation to provide opportunities to see how we can navigate challenging circumstances, which have become topics we cannot avoid. Although, by reading a further in-depth conversation, we hope that our differing perspectives and insights can help you not only navigate these challenges but also put yourself in the best position to make a positive impact. Below are the four Critical Conversation topics and dialogues composed in this book.

- **Critical Topic 1:** Suicide Prevention and Mental Health - How Can Teachers Navigate this Topic with their Students in Their Classroom?
- **Critical Topic 2:** Critical Race Theory vs. Culturally Relevant Teaching
- **Critical Topic 3:** Shifting and Toggling Through Multiple Classroom Settings? How can Teachers be Best Prepared to Teach in Online, Blended, and In-Person Settings?
- **Critical Topic 4:** Dealing with a Tragedy - How Can Teachers Navigate a Tragedy While Teaching?

Pre-Service vs. New Teacher vs. Experienced Teacher. Whether you're a pre-service teacher, a first-year teacher, or an experienced teacher, this book is a book for you. Depending on where you are in terms of experience may impact how you read this book. Ultimately, we want that to happen. We created this book to meet teachers where they are at in their teaching journey.

If you are a pre-service or new teacher, we recommend that your first read-through start at the beginning and work your way through to the end, as the tips and strategies can follow a sequence that will help you navigate your first few years in education. Then, for your second read-through, we suggest reviewing the table of contents and looking at various tips, strategies, and critical topics. Ultimately, this is an opportunity for growth, rethinking, and reaffirming what you already know and can do.

If you are an experienced teacher, we recommend using this book to review various topics you want to refresh. Review the table of contents to find tips, strategies, and Critical Conversations that may fit what you want to expand your teacher toolkit further. Additionally, like pre-service and new teachers, you may be experiencing a situation where one of the tips, strategies and Critical Conversations can further provide insight and support as you navigate that experience in your classroom and school.

Diversity, Inclusion, and Equity Lens

We must celebrate all our students in the classroom, at the desks, or on the board. We want everyone to feel that they belong within our classroom community. Most importantly, we want the best possible opportunities for all students. As the four of us were writing the book, we realized that we want new and experienced teachers to keep a significant demographic point in mind: American classrooms are evolving. Schaffer (2021) pointed out that our classrooms are becoming increasingly racially diverse, and the teaching force is still predominantly white. We also want teachers to keep in mind this point: we do not have your experiences. We have our own experiences, but we want to support and promote the voices of students and teachers as advocates and agents of change.

We recognize our limited experiences, but we want our readers to know that each of the following 50 tips is written with all students, localities, and characteristics in mind. The four authors have experienced work in a wide range of regions, school districts, and community locations. We have worked with students from many diverse backgrounds and support what Cross (1989) explains: each of us as human beings is always learning, and we should ensure that we ask questions, do our research, and learn. We must, as educators, assume that we do not know and implement the work required to better understand our students' and colleagues' cultures.

We felt many great resources could accompany you on this journey concerning diversity, inclusion, and equity. If you feel you want more information, our team recommends you explore the following resources:

- Emdin, C. (2016). For White folks who teach in the hood... and the rest of y'all too: Reality pedagogy and urban education. Beacon Press.
- Kendi, I. X. (2019). How to be an antiracist. One World.
- Landsman, J., & Lewis, C. W. (2006). White teachers, diverse classrooms: A guide to building inclusive schools, promoting high expectations, and eliminating racism. Stylus Publishing, LLC.
- Delano-Oriaran, O. O., & Meidl, T. D. (2013). Critical conversations: Developing White teachers for diverse classrooms. Journal of Praxis in Multicultural Education, 7(1), 1.
- Howard, G. R. (2016). We can't teach what we don't know: White teachers, multiracial schools. Teachers College Press.
- Gruenewald, D. A. (2014). Place-based education in the global age. Routledge.

We want to support and promote the voices of all students, educators, and communities. We hope you envision yourself doing the same as you read our book and think and reflect upon each tip and practice through a diversity, inclusion, and equity lens.

Ready Set Go - #50TeacherTipsBook

Use the hashtag **#50TeacherTipsBook** as well as our website www.50teachertips.com to connect with readers of this book as well as the authors. Our goal is to not only provide these tips, strategies, and Critical Conversations but also learn together, connect, and be #BetterTogether. Local and global support, established through our collective learning community, is critical to sustainable teaching. We want to support you all in your journeys beyond what's shared in this book. Please harness this network and reach out. Educators, including us, will be happy to communicate with you and help you navigate teaching in our ever-changing world.

Educators, including us, will be happy you are beginning your journey in teaching or are further along in your career, we cannot wait to join you on that journey. Our experiences, research, and a collection of experiences from our local and global professional learning network make up the many tips, strategies, and Critical Conversations encompassing this book. We wrote this book to curate these experiences and conversations to help you navigate our ever-changing field. Ultimately, we want to support you along your journey and provide tips and strategies along with your learned experiences to make teaching the best experience possible as well as sustainable and authentic. It will allow you to be your best for yourself, your family, and your students. As everyone embarks on their personalized journey, we hope you can all connect with us and share your experiences and insight throughout your experience in education.

As you read this book, we hope you take these tips, strategies, and Critical Conversations and apply them to your practice. Teaching requires us to take risks and to practice over and over again strategies that not only help our students learn but also for us to create sustainable routines. In all honesty, teaching is hard. However, think less is more, take time to reflect, and take care of yourself. These principles will help you take your knowledge, lived experiences, and hopefully, these tips and strategies and amplify them. We will be here along the way and cannot wait to see where your practice will take you and what amazing things will happen in your classroom and life.

SECTION 1: THE ANTICIPATION AND FIRST INTERACTION

July   **August**

September

"Start where you are. Use what you have. Do what you can." - Arthur Ashe

Section 1: The Anticipation and First Interaction

This first section gives tips to help you work through the anticipation of the new school year. For some of you, graduation just happened. You subbed until now or may have only student taught, and you now have your contract in your hand. You might experience a traditional summer of job searching, relocation, and working on adding some money. You might also have started taking graduate classes, as you want to prepare yourself for your first year of teaching.

Remember one critical point: most hiring happens in the late summer. Don't panic. Breathe. After you have sent out applications, resumes, fingerprinting, certification applications, and you may have a couple of rounds of interviews, including a phone screening. You may also teach a demo lesson- to students or the hiring committee. Remember, you should try your best, but if you do not get hired immediately, **do not panic**. Here are some tips we think you need to keep in mind.

Tips and Strategy Entries 1-16

Tip 1: Thinking Less is More in all you do.

When we were new teachers, we faced many things that sometimes became overwhelming. When we began our careers in teaching, we were inundated with things that could, at times, become overwhelming. For example, we spent too much time grading, preparing for Individualized Education Plan (IEP) meetings, worrying about communicating with each family, and lesson planning. All aspects as previously mentioned are essential for success, but we as teachers tend to be perfectionists and spend too much time trying to perfect each of them. It is essential to do your best and to provide the best product. Still, we know that if we had a "less is more" mindset and focused on how to make habits that made these responsibilities significantly more efficient, we would stress less, have more time, and enjoy working directly with students. Sam shares that as a first-year teacher, she focused more on planning curriculum and content than building relationships with her students during the first few days of classes. During the first few days, she wishes she would have spent more time getting to know her students; she does that now with her preservice teachers.

We have to make thousands of split-second decisions as teachers throughout the day. It takes a lot of energy, and it can ultimately be exhausting. Therefore, you should think about how you teach. Additionally, we must think of how we can teach with the mindset that "less is more" because teachers are prone to overthinking and complicating what they are doing in their instruction, routines, and communication with students and families.

Thinking less is more is undoubtedly a loaded statement. It all comes down to teaching habits, how we approach them systematically, and how many we choose to focus on. Focusing first on our habits, we can develop a list of concrete responsibilities, routines, instructional strategies, and communication mechanisms. Identifying our top three habits will illustrate how we can focus on these categories. Our ultimate goal will be for you to begin to break down this topic and determine which teaching habits you will focus on versus others that aren't as important and won't significantly affect your relationships or instruction with students. This idea is fundamental. Determining which habits to employ in your practice is the most challenging part. Let's walk you through a step-by-step process to help you do this in your practice.

- **Step 1.** Make a list of five to eight areas where you spend most of your time. Think of these as buckets that you fill each day.
- **Step 2.** Write down your top three priorities in each of these areas.
- **Step 3.** Consider how you completed each task. Consider how long it will take you to complete each task or what you will need to complete each one.
- **Step 4.** Determine which tasks are necessary and which are not and eliminate unneeded tasks.
- **Step 5.** As for the remaining tasks in each area, think about how you can make each one efficient in terms of time and how effective they are in completing the task. Our ability now to automate many of our mundane tasks, which are not directly teaching to students synchronously, has dramatically increased.

- **Step 6.** You should write down your list of five to eight areas and the daily tasks you have evaluated. By the end of this activity, you should have a much smaller list than what you had previously.

A good example is always appreciated. Matt shares a step-by-step example of how to do this below.

Figure 1.1

Matt's Teaching Tasks Using Think Less is More After Step 1-6

Instruction

- Warm-up/Formative Assessment: Quick Write, Error Analysis
- Guided Practice: Think, Pair, Share, Checking for Understanding, Gradual Release
- Independent Practice: Station Rotation/Center, Student Choice board
- Assessment: Competency-based and self-assessment

Planning

- One Hour a Day – 30 minutes before school
- Using a Google Doc with Hyperlinks

Organization

- Google Drive for documents
- Google Classroom for assignments, announcements

Communication

- Google Voice for texting and calls
- Email
- Office Hours

Assessment/Grading

- Once a week, grade via a rubric
- Feedback will be given whole class and individually

Technology

- Use Google Classroom as a learning management system
- Utilize Zoom for any synchronous online instruction and meetings
- Pear Deck for direct instruction and active learning

Go ahead and complete this activity for yourself using Figure 1.2 above as the model. Reflect on the following areas as you develop this, and remember that less is more.

Figure 1.2

Your Teaching Tasks Using Think Less is More After Steps 1-6

Instruction

-
-
-

Planning

-
-
-

Organization

-
-
-

Communication

-
-
-

Assessment/Grading

-
-
-

Technology

-
-
-

After completing this activity, you will be able to think less is more in your practice as an educator. As with anything, responsibilities change over time, as do the associated tasks. Your list might also change depending on where you are in your life. By completing this activity monthly or bi-annually, you can take things off your plate and think about how you teach, plan, assess, organize, communicate, and so much more.

Becoming a reflective educator and focusing on everything you are responsible for in your position will help you set boundaries. Think about how you complete many of the tasks you do each day and develop sustainable practices to help you not only now but also in the future.

Activity Putting Tip #1 Into Action: I Used to Think vs. Now I Think

Directions: What did you "used to think" and outline what you "now think" after reading this tip and associated strategies to support your teaching practice? Share your thoughts with your PLN with the hashtag **#50TeacherTipsBook**.

I Used to Think	Now I Think

Tip 2: Sparking Joy with Bell Ringers

The beginning of a class is an essential part of it. What happens when students enter your classroom or log in to your virtual space? A teacher's routine (or lack of one) determines how each period of the school day begins. An effective routine makes learning and transitioning from classes easier. Alternatively, a chaotic and unorganized start leads to distraction, confusion, or a lack of student interest. It would help if you had a clear, consistent, and joyful routine to maximize instructional time.

How do we start a class effectively? If you have ever sat in front of an essay and spent hours considering what the first line should be, you know how difficult it is. Most educators have spent years learning to deliver content effectively and engage in pedagogical strategies but have spent little time contemplating how to transition into that part of the day. As a result, the start of class becomes a barrier to the teacher's success, interrupting their lesson before it can begin.

It is crucial to establish a routine when you begin your class. In many pre-service teaching programs, your instructor tells you that a bell ringer is a key to success. Students must do this each day at the start of class as a class activity. It is important to note, however, that the existence of a bell ringer does not guarantee smooth transitions. It can even become a distraction from your lesson. For this reason, we must understand the purpose of our warm-up activity.

Kevin says that at the beginning of his career, he tried out every strategy to start the class on a positive note. One of his first ideas was to dive right into the lesson. It quickly became apparent that it was unrealistic since students would still be filtering in, morning announcements would still buzz on the speakers, and questions and comments would fill the air with noise and confusion. It became clear that his students needed bell ringer activities. In the wake of that failed experiment, he began implementing bell ringer activities daily. Through college textbooks and veteran teachers, he developed specific workbook activities. The class would solve a grammatical problem in their journals daily. Then, he would grade each grammar problem they attempted as a warm-up activity. He would then correct the answers together on the projector. Neat. Easy. Boring.

Kevin was not ready to change until a few years had passed. He had a structure to his classroom, so students knew what to do as soon as they walked in. The warm-ups, however, were frequently complained about, and a complete disconnect between the warm-up and the lesson. This made transitioning difficult. As a result, it became a barrier students had to overcome before they could learn. Kevin realized he had misunderstood the purpose of a bell ringer. His initial definition of a bell ringer was: "an introductory activity that emphasizes a standard of learning for student growth." This was not a good transition since it became a separate lesson.

Kevin also changed how he approached starting a class by changing his definition. Now, it reads: "A bell ringer is a great way to engage student curiosity, foster positive relationships, and ignite joy." Kevin's pedagogy changed profoundly as a result of this new definition. There was laughter and exploration at the start of each day. Those who resisted class found themselves enjoying it and wondering what we would do next. As they rushed to class, they hoped they wouldn't miss their favorite part of the day - our warm-up activity. Preparedness and timeliness are powerful characteristics of a successful transition activity.

Although the bell ringer activities varied many times, these three elements ensured that he got the most out of the first 5-10 minutes of each class:

- Clear - Students can begin the bell ringer activity without me. It is clear to them what needs to be done, why it is being done, and how students should do it.
- Consistent - The bell ringer is a regular part of the schedule and doesn't change. Students can count on it being a consistent and structured part of the schedule. Even if there are changes, they are consistent (e.g., new quarterly warm-ups).
- Sparks Joy - The bell ringer addresses students' interests and passions. This part allows them to be curious and intrigued. This promotes dialogue and discussion.

The bell ringer does not mention anything about the content. This is on purpose. The purpose of the first transitional activity is to prepare the learner for learning rather than for particular content. This does not mean that you cannot use content in your course. Just that it is not the focus of this activity, it would be even better to integrate warm-ups into your course content. Don't lose sight of the actual purpose of the bell ringer.

Consider how you want to begin each class period. Consider whether it will spark joy in your students. Engage in dialogue with your students during the first few minutes of class, learn their interests, and humanize your classroom. Students will be likelier to arrive on time, be present in the classroom, and engage in the material.

Activity Putting Tip #2 Into Action: The 3 C's of Bell Ringers

Directions:

- In the space below, jot down your ideas regarding the 3 C's of bell ringers.
- Be as specific as possible so you can brainstorm ways to implement this strategy in the classroom.
- Share your thoughts with your PLN with the hashtag **#50TeacherTipsBook.**

- **Clear** - Students can begin the bell ringer activity without me. It is clear to them what needs to be done, why it is being done, and how they should do it.

- **Consistent** - The bell ringer is a regular part of the schedule and doesn't change. Students can count on it being a consistent and structured part of the schedule. Even if there are changes, they are consistent (e.g., new quarterly warm-ups).

- **Sparks Collaboration and Joy:** The bell ringer addresses students' interests and passions. This allows them to be curious and intrigued. This promotes dialogue and discussion.

Tip 3: Reflecting on Routines in Digital and In-person Classrooms

We live in a digital and in-person world. Both students and adults will have to navigate these ever-changing spheres. Our spheres in our lives are ever-expanding in how much they have become. We live in classrooms without boundaries. We have opened Pandora's box. Before 2020, we were well on our way to having classrooms in K-12 that have both digital and physical spaces. COVID-19 caused an exponential rise in both digital and physical classrooms.

As a result, many of our classrooms operate with routines, instruction, and community within multiple classroom settings. For teachers to succeed in modern classrooms, they must develop routines for digital and in-person settings.

Routines are essential to having successful classrooms. Routines encompass every aspect of classroom activities, from entering to exiting, transitioning from activities, instructional sequences, gaining access to materials and resources, and communicating with each other. This includes not only our physical classroom, but also our digital classroom spaces. Therefore, in our modern classrooms, we need to have routines built to transcend both spaces for our students. As a result, a number of these routines encompassing both spaces will be discussed, and strategies will be outlined for navigating both spaces in your classroom.

Digital Classroom Routines

How do we go about creating digital routines? Similar to in-person classroom routines, it all comes down to teacher clarity and scaffolding directions over time until they become habits. We must practice routines almost every day if we want them to become embedded in a class.

As a result, to get our students to use an EdTech tool or an LMS (i.e., Canvas, Google Classroom, Seesaw, etc.) the way we want them to, they must use them nearly every day. If not, they may forget how to use it.

Teacher clarity, scaffolding, and repetition are essential for establishing routines. We must have clear instructions on using an EdTech tool and an LMS. Starting from turning on the device and going to the application through the web or an application shortcut, this route must be established, broken down, and modeled for students.

Another example would be to have students learn how to use a tool to create content. For example, if students are expected to use Google Workspace applications such as Docs, Slides, Draw, and Sheets, they should be guided through how to do so consistently. Routines may involve how students use the top toolbar of each application to write and create content. Routines can also include how students turn in work for feedback and how they review feedback.

Routines online are just as important as those in person. Think about how you can apply digital routines to in-person and online classroom experiences to make them transient. Please keep it simple by only using three to five EdTech tools consistently. Too many tools and routines surrounding them are overwhelming and ineffective. It is possible to introduce new tools and routines over time, but this should be very rare.

The Learning Management Systems - Digital and In-Person Routines

Learning management systems (LMS) allow instructors to store instructional materials in one place and facilitate classroom activities in-person and online. Routines are needed to enable students to access the LMS, open the lesson, and complete the task. Students can use them online as well as in-person. These routines can look similar even though they may look different in fully digital online settings than in-person. When students enter the classroom in-person, they have the choice of retrieving their computers from the cart or pulling out their computers. They are then instructed to turn it on and go to the class's LMS to pull up the day's lesson. To access the LMS online, students would follow the same steps, except they would not need to enter the classroom and retrieve their devices. It might be different in-person versus when students access the class online from home. The slides explain the lesson for the day. They may not see the class's daily instructions until they fully log into the LMS and access the daily lesson materials or join the synchronous online class sessions where their teacher has shared their screen containing the lesson instructions. Can you see how digital and in-person routines can blend despite similarities and differences? We must develop routines encompassing digital and in-person tools in the modern classroom.

In-Person Classroom Routines

The teacher must clarify, scaffold, and reinforce in-person classroom routines similarly to digital routines. Work through with your students.

- Process of entering class
- Process of exiting class
- Expectations for collaborative and independent work
- Instructional strategies
- Structuring your lessons to norms related to how students treat each other and establish and maintain a positive learning community.

Several of these routines blend digital and in-person elements, enabling you to double-dip in how you teach them to your students and incorporate them into your daily class schedule.

How can we reinforce these routines? We must model them daily and positively reinforce them when our students can follow them. Instructional strategies also fall into this category, since they are routines facilitating learning. For example, teaching students an instructional sequence is a routine in itself. Think, write, pair, and share, for example, won't be as effective the first few times because it's new to our students. However, after practicing it and having it become one of your main strategies, students will see it as a routine, amplifying the strategy because students will do it more effectively over time.

Creating a culture around routines requires commitment. Building a community of learners where students treat each other well requires buy-in. Developing many routines may require them to be student-led, especially when beginning the year when classroom norms and establishing community are paramount to starting the year well. Ask students what an ideal classroom is in their opinion. Be democratic. Teachers must model how their ideas can become norms and routines. Having this element of student choice helps establish buy-in. Beyond this initial buy-in, we can continue to create more buy-in and community by providing opportunities to individually and collectively reflect on how things are going and providing a forum to voice these thoughts. Conducting circle check-ins periodically to check how students are doing with classroom routines and culture can be very advantageous because it engages students in a collaborative and communal dialogue. Ultimately, we must remember to ensure these moments of reflection and check-ins are established as routines. This piece will go a long way in building the needed buy-in from our students to maintain routines that go hand in hand with establishing and maintaining positive classroom cultures.

Combining Digital and In-person Classrooms

Classroom routines span all the realms where learning takes place. As mentioned before, our routines must blend, be transient, and flexible to be able to do this. Working with students on skills related to:

- Accessing and using our EdTech tools in-person and online at home
- Building positive learning communities in-person and online
- Navigating our digital and physical classrooms to access content, resources, and communication tools
- Developing routines related to student accountability, our routines must marry these classroom spaces.

We will never go back to providing instruction within solely in-person classroom spaces. Our classrooms have become not just four walls. They have become knocked down and become classrooms without boundaries.

Routines will make or break your classroom culture and instruction. We must be strategic and intentional with creating our routines for in-person and online classroom spaces. These realms make up modern classrooms, and the differences between each of these settings will continue to blur over time. Regardless of how experienced they are, teachers must navigate these settings and ensure students know how to access the instruction and content they are receiving. By being transparent with our routines, modeling, and scaffolding, and through repetition, routines can be established and maintained. As long as these principles are held, you will have a level of success in developing routines regardless of what setting you are trying to implement them in.

Activity Putting Tip #3 Into Action: Developing Routines

Directions: Reflect upon digital and in-person routines for your class. How will you create student buy-in? How will you develop and model these routines? Share your thoughts with your PLN with the hashtag **#50TeacherTipsBook**.

In-Person Routine	Digital Learning Routine

Tip 4: Remembering Your Why

Knowing and understanding your why is crucial for a teacher. An example of a why is the statement in this context is "why did you become a teacher?" You need to be able to refer to it daily and know that you are on the right track. You can stay grounded in your learning and growth as a teacher by knowing your why. Let's work on defining your why. Let's start by finding a quiet place and setting both physically and mentally. Use the space below in the activity to reflect on the questions.

Once you have written out your why statement, you should put it in a place you can refer to daily. Know that your why is not set in stone. It changes and grows as you do. Understanding your why gives you a sense of direction. It gives you direction in your teaching career. Understanding your why gives you your vision and mission statement that you can refer to. When you are faced with a decision, we encourage you to reflect on your why.

To keep your why front and center, you can create an image on the desktop of your phone or computer. Or keep it on a sticky note on your computer or desk.

Activity Putting Tip #4 Into Action: Your Why

Directions: Consider your answers to these questions. Share your WHY statement with your PLN with the hashtag **#50TeacherTipsBook**.

Why did you decide to become an educator?	
Are you a teacher because of who inspired you? If so, who? How did this person (or persons) impact your teaching story?	
What do you enjoy most about teaching this subject?	
What do you enjoy about the age or grade you teach?	
In what way do you hope to make an impact on your class?	
How would you describe the atmosphere in your classroom?	

Tip 5: Preventing Burnout from the Beginning

Burnout dominates pop culture and the media. Regardless of where you live or how long you have worked in education, you have no doubt heard about burnout. However, it is rarely mentioned in pre-service teacher preparation programs or research. Understanding burnout is essential for all new teachers.

Burnout can be better understood if we look at its beginnings. The term burnout was coined in 1974 by Herbert Freudenberger, a psychologist working in a free clinic. He often worked with recovering drug addicts who were "burned out" after detoxing. As he worked, he noticed his staff (and even himself) exhibited similar symptoms to those of the addicts detoxing. Due to the similarities, he called it burnout. Taking burnout to a new level, Christina Maslach (2017) defined three categories: emotional exhaustion, depersonalization, and personal accomplishments. Burnout conversations typically center on emotional exhaustion, but these other two elements also contribute to burnout. Personal accomplishment refers to the rewards you perceive from your work, while depersonalization refers to cynicism and isolation. Burnout results from pouring yourself into your work without receiving the rewards, accomplishments, or impact you had hoped for, leaving you cynical about your career.

One of the most challenging aspects of burnout is its lack of clearly identifiable markers. There is no way to test for burnout in a doctor's office. Symptoms vary and can occur at different times. Other root causes can also cause symptoms of burnout. Burnout operates on a scale, so it is impossible to say if you have it. Many people experience burnout on different levels. Due to the lack of a clear indicator of burnout, it is important to monitor yourself using Maslach's three elements. This will help you to keep a realistic view of your burnout. You may feel emotionally exhausted by working hard to impact students' lives and consider yourself burned out. However, you may also feel a sense of accomplishment and a desire to continue learning and collaborating with other educators. A rewarding purpose drives the fatigue you feel. The feeling is not necessarily one of burnout (although you should monitor the fatigue and work to balance work and energy).

As well as following Maslach's indicators, it is crucial to be aware of your physical and emotional health. Burnout is associated with many symptoms of varying severity. It is therefore essential to recognize patterns. Are you frequently ill with fatigue, colds, and cases of flu? Are you experiencing regular bouts of anxiety, frustration, or depression that weren't frequent before you started teaching? Burnout may be the cause of chronic illness. You should always consult a medical professional to rule out other possibilities.

The easiest way to treat burnout is to be proactive. After years of being burnt out, it is tough to return from it. Apply these practices instead to fend off burnout and prevent it from the start.

- **Self-Efficacy -** Feelings of competence and confidence will help you overcome burnout. Low levels of self-efficacy become a breeding ground for burnout, as self-doubt and a constant feeling of "not doing enough" will lead to overworking yourself.
- **Mentorship -** Your school may assign you a mentor at the beginning of your teaching career. Mentorship is a foundational practice for fending off burnout. This does not mean that every mentor is qualified to help you. You should make the most out of your working relationship with your mentor, but you should also continue looking for additional mentors inside and outside your school setting.
- **Healthy Habits -** By nature, burnout accumulates and becomes more challenging to deal with the longer it operates within you. Healthy habits, like exercising, nutrition, and sleep, empower you to confront feelings of burnout. Without robust health and high levels of energy, slight feelings of burnout will have a much more significant impact on you.
- **Resilience -** This career path will challenge you. There will be days that feel easy and others that feel impossible. Resilience is crucial to overcoming the difficulties and obstacles that await you. Building resilience will make burnout less likely and allow you to bounce back easier if it does grab hold of you.

All those who enter service careers are at risk of burnout, which is silent, mysterious, and dangerous. Please don't assume it won't happen to you or that it doesn't require your attention. When you work on burnout prevention methods early in your career, you will have a more satisfying, healthy, and safe career.

Activity Putting Tip #5 Into Action: Monitoring Your Teacher Burnout

Directions: Please write down and commit to one step in each of the categories below to prevent burnout. Use the hashtag **#50TeacherTipsBook** to share your thoughts with your PLN.

Improving Self-Efficacy:

Finding & Utilizing A Mentor:

A Healthy Habit You Will Add/Improve On:

A Resilience-Building Practice:

Tip 6: Creating a Not-to-Do List Before Creating a To-Do List

A series of things drive teachers throughout the school day that they have to complete. From planning and teaching to meetings and email, there are many things we will have to complete throughout the day. One way to navigate these facets is to create a to-do list. To-do lists aim to illustrate what you need to complete for that day, week, or month to complete the tasks you feel you need to complete to succeed in your teaching position.

To-do lists can be written down on paper or done digitally. A planner, Google Keep, calendar, or piece of paper are generally the mediums for to-do lists. Matt shares that he preferred a digital to-do list because he tended to look at his phone more than a specific piece of paper. He would write down the top three things to do each day. Then, when Matt completed each task, he crossed it off his phone. Sam shares that she keeps both digital and a paper planner. Specifically, she uses One Note to share her daily list of to-dos and prioritizes daily. She uses the paper planner for oversized picture items and plans. A to-do list helps you navigate and be successful in the classroom. By writing things down, you become more productive. However, there is a caveat. Sometimes, you may take on additional obligations and tasks during the school day. Occasionally, teaching to-do list grew exponentially, resulting in feeling overwhelmed.

Matt shares that sometimes, his to-do list got so big that he had to work for an entire week to catch up. He shares that working as a Special Education teacher, pressing deadlines such as drafting parts of an Individualized Education Plan, conducting goal progress, and communicating with students and parents on top of teaching, created an enormous amount of stress. What began to help alleviate this stress and the overwhelming feeling of the to-do list was to begin to create boundaries in his work.

To maintain the to-do list and create boundaries, one thing you can do is create a not-to-do list. This list comprises all the non-negotiables to you, which allow you to set in writing what you are not going to do that will get you away from the primary responsibilities in the classroom.

Below, look at the example not-to-do list in Figure 6.1 that may help you create your own. Then, use Figures 6.2 and 6.3 to create your not-to-do list. Review each box in Figure 6.2 and then complete. Following completing Figure 6.2, create your final not-do list in the activity below.

Figure 6.1

Example of Matt's Not-to-Do List

Not-To-Do List
1. Email during the instructional hours of a school day.
2. Say "No" more than "Yes" when asked for something beyond teaching and planning.
3. Ever take work home.
4. Grade more than one weekly assignment to enter in the grade book.
Informal conferences or calls with students and families will not go beyond 15 minutes.

Figure 6.2

Creating a Not-To-Do List - A Process of Elimination

My Current To-Do List	What is Draining Me?
	What Does Not Need To Get Done?
	My Current Responsibilities
	Responsibilities of Others

Starting with three to five items is likely the best in creating your not-to-do list since those are your non-negotiables as a teacher. You can add as many not-to-do's on your list as they are non-negotiable and out of your scope of work. As a result of this list, you are creating a set of habits you will not cross.

Along with your to-do list, have your not-to-do list on your phone, in a Google Doc, or at a desk in your office or classroom. Therefore, you can see them side by side and evaluate whether the following items on your to-do list may violate your not-to-do list. Hopefully, over time with this in place, it may be one factor alleviating your stress levels while teaching.

Activity Putting Tip #6 Into Action: Square, Circle, and Triangle

Directions: After reading this tip, write down your thoughts in each shape. First, what is one thing that squared with your thinking? Next, what is one question still encapsulating your mind? Last, what are three points you'll remember? Share your thoughts with your PLN with the hashtag **#50TeacherTipsBook**.

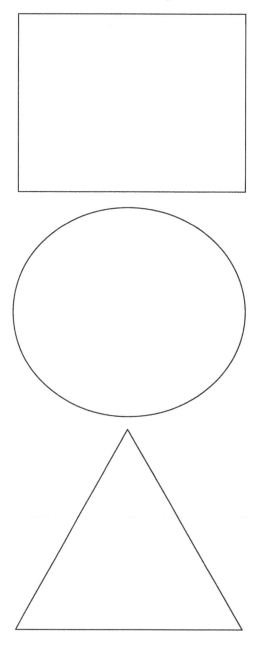

Tip 7: Saying Goodbye to Reviewing the Syllabus on Day 1

As Kevin shared earlier, we need to start our day and year off with relationships. We can't just dive into content right away. To that end, we wanted to share the benefits of starting your year by building relationships. She shares that in years past, she would have her students go over the syllabus point by point, but now she doesn't even go over the syllabus on day three. Instead, she builds relationships with her students that help her students and herself to work through the semester together.

Establishing relationships with your students from the beginning allows you to cultivate respect and rapport. We respect their background and experiences because we recognize that there is much more to our students than what they display in school. Our students need to know that we genuinely care about and believe in them. We encourage you to learn about the families and cultures of your students. Get to know students' interests, what they love to do, where they've traveled, where they've lived, etc. Here are some ways to start building relationships with your students (some even before the semester begins).

- Create a shared playlist of music for everyone. You can play the music as they enter or exit the class. Or you can play it while students are working at their desks. Another idea is to use the music during transitions. For example, the students have until the song ends to prepare for their next class activity or lesson.
- Greet students by name: their names, how to pronounce their name, and their preferred pronouns. The benefits of this are twofold: one, students know that they are valued and appreciated, and two, it lets them know they are in the right classroom, easing some stress.
- Students can post digital sticky notes on Padlet, a virtual bulletin board. The notes include text, images, links, and other digital content. Padlet boards can be created and shared with students for engagement.
- You can easily create these forms in Google or Microsoft. Send students a quick survey to get to know them better. It can be helpful at the beginning of the school year when you plan assignments and want to know what students are doing outside school.
- Students can introduce themselves through collaborative drawings on a whiteboard using the Microsoft Whiteboard app, Nearpod or Peardeck, or the Whiteboard.fi website. It is possible to share your screen so everyone can see each other's drawings or keep them private. Students can also play Pictionary in small groups using one of these tools.
- With Adobe Express, you can create a variety of activities to deliver content to students and have them create their content. One of these activities is creating an "about me" video. Adobe Express is excellent because it walks you through the whole process step-by-step. You can upload your photos and videos. In addition, you can add audio to your video to explain ideas and concepts.
- Flip (Flip) - This is a video platform that you can use to share videos of yourself and have students send you videos in response. You can set up different prompts for your students to respond to, and they can use video, text, and emojis to respond to the prompt. Students enter a code, join a grid, and respond to other students. The system is straightforward to use, share, and record. Another fun fact about Flip is the ability to record your screen, use a board, and draw on the board with your audio support playing in the background.

Activity Putting Tip #7 Into Action: Building Relationships Blueprint

Directions: Brainstorm some ways you can start and continue to build relationships with your students throughout the school year. Share your thoughts with your PLN with the hashtag **#50TeacherTipsBook**.

Tip 8: Classroom Management - Four Ways to Manage Your Classroom Better

The topic of classroom management may dominate the first few years of a teaching career. Kevin was given fewer than three books and six mandatory classroom management strategies to use in his first week as a teacher. It became the focus of every observation and every growth plan target. Talk about stress. Nothing piles on anxiety like an overwhelming, persistent presence of a challenging part of a job that is often outside one's control. Considering the variety of strategies available, this section will not debate what works and doesn't. We have seen various strategies work, sometimes contradictory methods, if done well and according to the teacher's strengths. Research can provide hints as to what strategies will likely have a higher or lower impact, but we cannot tell you what will work well in your specific context. As a result, this section examines a simple aspect of classroom management: navigating and hopefully reducing your students' stress by setting up norms and routines in your classroom to create a positive culture and climate.

Classroom management is establishing and maintaining norms and routines for the culture and climate of your classroom. While management is often used, you are essentially creating expectations through norms and developing routines relating to academics, social scenarios, behavior, community interaction, and a range of positive and negative consequences for following the norms and routines. Ultimately, we will also formulate and navigate the relationship we have collectively with our class and individual students. This tip aims to break down several norms and routines you can implement in your classroom. We want to make a very complex set of norms and routines and navigate our relationships with students as efficiently as possible. Several other tips, such as the tip on restorative justice, can be integrated into what is discussed within this tip. Also, we must consider our instruction and the strategies we integrate into our lessons as they all require norms and routines to activate and implement with our students. Throughout this tip, we will discuss several principles to get you started with classroom management and how we can develop these norms and routines. Students' experiences and skills in your class will be critical in navigating these spheres that encompass their interactions with others and future work.

Principles for Navigating Classroom Management

- Healthy-living will not be the teacher you hope to be through constant stress and worry. If you're losing sleep, working late, or panicking throughout the day, your classroom management will not be sustainable. Whatever strategies you implement, they must grant peace and calm to your classroom, or it will rule you. Try these three strategies to destress your classroom management and make it an enjoyable rather than frustrating process.

- Simplify - Your class rules should be straightforward for students to understand and follow. Many well-intentioned teachers have class rule lists that go beyond 20 items. Each rule may be purposeful, but the problem lies in the complexity. What student will keep all 20 items on the top of their head every minute in class? Combine rules, pair them down, and simplify the language. Focus on your top priorities and ensure students can actively see that focus. If you only have 2-3 rules to check on, you will regain the freedom of your time and energy to spend on teaching. Otherwise, you will find yourself constantly navigating a checklist in your head to ensure there are no rule-breakers.

- Clarify- Do your students know exactly how to follow your rules and procedures? A topic that feels clear to you may be muddled with someone else. Ask any pre-K teacher who has taught students about personal space. One student may believe that to be six feet or greater, while another might think it simply means "breathing on you but not actively touching you." Whatever you expect of students should be clear enough for them to follow, explain, and give the reasoning for why the expectation exists. Nothing is more frustrating than stopping a lesson to clarify a procedure you believed your students knew and supported.

- Ditch Perfect - You've simplified your class rules. Then, you spent time clarifying each rule, habit, and procedure for the class to ensure everyone was on the same page. The final step to destress your classroom management is to abandon your expectation of perfection. Yes, we want our rules obeyed and our procedures followed. However, if you demand perfection from all students, you will quickly find that classroom management will dominate your teaching time. Students will make mistakes. If you plan to uphold perfection, you will be constantly busy, worried, and anxious about spotting the "problems."

Implementing these three steps will not guarantee a well-organized classroom management system. There are many strategies to consider and a plethora of ideas that may work for you. However, these three steps will ensure that you do not make classroom management your most significant stressor. Simplify, clarify, and drop your expectations of perfection to bring balance to your career and remove the anxieties of classroom management.

Classroom Norms and Routines Make-Up Classroom Management

Many classroom norms and routines are essential for our physical classroom spheres. They all relate to navigating the classroom throughout the lesson and day and establishing behavior norms and community. You should walk into your classroom with an idea of how you would like to set these norms, but discussing, debating, and implementing them with your students may also be wise. Don't be a rule enforcer. Instead, be a classroom facilitator. Consider the following elements as a beginning to your classroom norms:

- Establishing Behavior Norms and Community
- Entering and Exiting the classroom
- Transitioning from one activity to another
- Stations/Centers
- Use of Music for Transitions
- Chunk and Scaffolds to Introduce Strategies
- Methods for Collecting and Passing Out Assignments
- Physical Movement (sharpening pencils, gathering materials, movement breaks, etc.)
- Bathroom Procedures

Activity Putting Tip #8 Into Action: Classroom Management

Directions: Use this space to brainstorm three expectations that are clearly stated. How will you model these rules and expectations to your students? How will you create student buy-in? Share your thoughts with your PLN with the hashtag **#50TeacherTipsBook**.

Tip 9: Decision Tree - Self-Advocacy

You need to know how to advocate for yourself throughout your career. We have recommended the following decision tree for novice teachers facing the question, "Is this worth it?" Sometimes, you need to let go of a bother. Often, we recommend letting go of the small things. But other times, if small things are built, or a significant issue unfolds, you should deal with it head-on. We recommend you duplicate this page for future use. Understand that advocacy is not arrogance. Instead, it is an excellent way to identify what and how you want to create a positive working environment for yourself and your students. This is not an arrogance area but instead a self-preservation request. Also, you want continuous improvement thinking (CIT). The enemy of improvement is compliance.

A decision tree can help you identify ethical questions, create positive boundaries, and identify areas for concern. In teaching, you will make hundreds of decisions. You will face new, complicated, and recurring situations that you must think through. A decision tree will help you:

- identify the issue
- identify your concern
- identify other's stances/viewpoints
- identify possible decision routes
- identify a course of action

Seek advice, seek guidance, and seek a fair solution. Remember, you are learning. The most complex decisions you will make as a teacher involve other people's beliefs and ideas. Always apologize if you make a wrong decision, own it, and move on. Learning for the life of you is more critical than instantaneous perfection. A sample decision tree is on the next page you can use as your model to help you navigate times when self-advocacy may be needed.

Activity Putting Tip #9 Into Action: Advocating for Myself and Others

Directions: Use this space to respond to the questions below to help develop your self-advocacy skills. Share your thoughts with your PLN with the hashtag **#50TeacherTipsBook**.

What is bothering me?	
Why is it bothering me?	
What did I do?	
What did the other person(s) do?	
Who can I go to for help?	
Mentor (informal)	Supervisor (formal)
What are the actions recommended?	

Can I see myself implementing the suggestions?	
Does the situation still require action or addressing? If yes-> WHY?	If no-> I will live with it.
What are the action steps I need to take in order to solve the issue?	
What are potential positives?	
What are potential draw backs?	
What did I learn from this situation?	
What will I do next time?	

Tip 10: Working with Instructional Strategies to Help You Do More with Less

A teacher's bread and butter are instructional strategies. We use them to facilitate student learning. Essentially, they are research-based methodologies that aim to help students learn. You will be taught many instructional strategies during your pre-service years and career. The toolkit is constantly growing, and we have too many tools. Having a tool belt of effective strategies handy is good because you never know what kind of tool you'll need. Therefore, knowing many research-based strategies to implement in your classroom is effective and efficient.

When it comes to instructional strategies, we believe less is more. Focusing on five to eight strategies at a time that can be used throughout the entire lesson plan helps you become an expert in the strategies and keeps your students familiar with them. Ultimately, we want teachers and students to have a lighter cognitive load. Learning outcomes are affected by cognitive load, which refers to the amount of information that our working memory can process at one time (Lechy & Sweller, 1988; Sweller, 2008). Therefore, we must ensure that our strategies do not overwhelm our students' ability to process information. We do not want to provide too many instructions at once, talk too much through direct instruction, or make a task too hard or too easy. When thinking of the strategies we offer, consider how you can make them more effective with these variables in mind.

Instructional strategies are deliberate strategies that help us teach our students skills and content. Cognitive science explains how the brain takes in, organizes, and retrieves the information needed to complete tasks. In addition to transferring this knowledge and information to other topics, instructional strategies can be employed to build knowledge and retention of what has been learned. As a result of these actions, it may create opportunities for retrieval and application of this information across a broad range of tasks. Therefore, we need to be intentional about the instructional strategies we use in our classes.

Before we delve into five instructional strategies we recommend learning and implementing in the classroom, we want to suggest to you think less is more about instructional strategies. We can employ instructional strategies across the content and skills we teach without utilizing more than five of them. A toolkit of five to eight tools is ideal since they can be installed throughout the lesson and moved interchangeably. We will explain the five instructional strategies below by describing how they can be implemented at various lesson stages.

Modeling/Guided Practice: Modeling allows us to provide the steps to set the stage and demonstrate how to complete a task or solve a problem through a worked example. This means showing your students examples of completing the task or work problems. As you or a video demonstration models the example, you can have students work alongside you. You ensure students can see exactly what you are modeling. Each step is broken down and chunked.

Then, after one or two examples, students are asked to complete a task similar to that you modeled with your live support to provide feedback and check for understanding. This is called guided practice. For example, students would complete one or two similar problems in mathematics. Students may write an additional prompt in English or be asked to place proper grammar and punctuation in a sentence after discussing semicolons. The purpose is to provide guided practice and feedback before students are released to practice independently or collaboratively without as much teacher support.

Think, Pair, Share: Think, pair, and share is a strategy that can be done at any point within a lesson. It is a three-step strategy where students are presented with a problem to first think about and process. Then, after about 30 seconds to a minute to process the prompt or problem presented, students are asked to pair with a partner or small group (3-4 max) to discuss how they may answer the prompt or solve the problem. During the collaboration time, which can last anywhere from 3 to 10 minutes, you could include a list of protocols and prompts to ensure students are accountable for collaborating.

For example, you could include several prompts that partners or groups are asked to present to one another. After time has been provided for pairs or groups to solve or respond to the prompt or problem presented, several pairs are asked to present. Their solutions or responses are shared with the class, and the whole group analyzes them. Feedback by the teacher can be provided during this time as well as by fellow students. Think, pair, and share can be further amplified using Google Slides, Pear Deck, or Nearpod to make it more interactive and easier accessible for a teacher to sequence the strategy and provide students feedback.

If you are met with a room of silence after the students have thought about their responses and shared, try these steps:

- Share something that you learned from your partner
- Did you and your partner agree or disagree with each other? What did you learn?
- Share the strategy you and your partner discussed.
- Interleaving/Spaced Practice

Interleaving and spaced practice are strategies that can help students build skills and content knowledge more efficiently and effectively. Interleaving is essentially mixed practice, meaning a series of problems are mixed in content (Taylor & Rohrer, 2010). For example, in mathematics, you could have one or two problems that focus on adding fractions while the next problem focuses on solving a one or two-step equation. Another example could include practicing new vocabulary for a second language. The vocabulary would include not just one topic. Instead, the vocabulary practice would include mixing new vocabulary related to various topics (i.e., household, colors, verbs, short greeting phrases). Ultimately, through interleaving, when focusing on improving our skills in two or more areas that are separated tasks, we can improve our performance. Overall, we do not want to focus on a series of content and practice it all together as it limits our ability to improve our retention of new information. We acquire new skills and mastery faster when the content and practice are mixed.

Spaced practice provides opportunities to practice over time versus cramming the practice altogether simultaneously for students (Taylor & Rohrer, 2010). A great example is assigning only a few practice problems of content each night versus assigning fifty of the same types of practice problems that must be completed. This spaced practice involves multiple learning sessions, but each session is shorter. Over time multiple practice sessions result in a more robust long-term memory concerning the content learned by the student. Additionally, as you may have picked up, interleaving was inferred here. Spaced practice is best paired with interleaving as we want to practice a mixed assortment of problems over time versus cramming a mass of problems during one sitting.

Scaffolding and Gradual Release Similar to modeling and guided practice, scaffolding and gradual release allow your students to build their way up to mastery and become more independent from teacher support as they get closer to mastery. Scaffolding involves creating bite-sized learning chunks and supports for students to solve problems.

For example, for a writing activity, a graphic organizer can be used as a scaffold to help students place their evidence in an organized manner to answer a prompt. Or, for mathematics, scaffolds can be placed to help students see the steps needed to solve a problem. Scaffolds can also be placed in Project-Based Learning. Each step of the project, from the research to creating the student work product and how the project is presented, are scaffolds.

The gradual release goes hand in hand with scaffolds placed within your instruction. As a scaffold is placed, gradual release can occur when teacher-centered support decreases over time, and more responsibility is placed on the student to solve and complete the task. Also, note that gradual release occurs during modeling and guided practice, which goes hand in hand with both scaffolding and gradual release. Hopefully, after thinking about these strategies, you can see how they can all go together. Each of these strategies provides structured learning for students with varying levels of teacher support throughout the learning process.

Formative Assessment & Feedback Formative assessment is the opportunity to see how students are doing regarding the skill and content you are teaching them. As a result, teachers can then provide feedback on student progress to the entire class or individual students. A formative assessment can be one or two problems you would like them to complete at the beginning or end of class. It can be a written response to a prompt relating to a topic you're focusing on in class. Essentially, formative assessment can be utilized at any time to help you measure where your learning is at.

There are a variety of tools that can help you be on top of your formative assessment and feedback game. Using Google Slides, Pear Deck, Nearpod, Quizizz, Kahoot, and Flip, there are a variety of ways that can meet learners where they are at and in a variety of modalities to help you measure what they know and then provide feedback. Using an interactive slide like Pear Deck or Nearpod, you can see students' real-time responses to the formative assessment. Then, once students have provided their responses, you can give them direct feedback nearly instantaneously. This can be overt feedback directly to the class verbally. Or, covert comments can be written that individual students see, read, and then make an actionable change.

A student's learning is based on instructional strategies. The strategies mentioned here can be utilized within any classroom setting. Therefore, if you ever have to teach online, these strategies can be integrated into your synchronous and asynchronous lesson.

Additionally, these strategies can be integrated into almost every EdTech tool imaginable, which allows them to be adjustable and malleable in what you would like to do in your classroom. Last, they are easy to learn and can be used as the foundation of your instructional tool kit. They are strategies to build upon with a "think less is more" mindset as you become more comfortable using these instructional strategies in your classroom.

Figure 10.1

Consider the five instructional strategies presented above. How will you use these strategies in your classroom?

Instructional Strategy	Notes / Ideas
Modeling/Guided Practice	
Think, Pair, Share	
Interleaving/Spaced Practice	

Scaffolding and Gradual Release	
Formative Assessment & Feedback	

Activity Putting The Tip #10 Into Action Activity: Designing Instructional Strategies

Directions: After reading this tip, write your thoughts in each space based on each prompt. Share your thoughts with your PLN with the hashtag **#50TeacherTipsBook**.

Write Down Three Instructional Strategies You Want to Implement
What Will Each Strategy Look Like in Your Classroom?
What Are the Necessary Steps Needed to Make Them a Reality in Your Classroom?

Tip 11: Working with Parents, Guardians, and Families

Education is a collaborative process between the child, the family (or guardians), the teacher, and the community. No one does the job alone. Each team member needs to contribute their best efforts and intentions to the child's education. Each group's level of expertise and training affects their actions and intentions. Professional educators may feel alone in our daily implementation struggles, but many parents also feel anxiety. Some assume the role through intention and adopt or foster, but most parents are created when their baby is born.

Even though parents have a position on education, the world has changed since they left secondary school and became parents ten or so years ago. Over the past decade, education has changed drastically, even compared to the "picture" in parents' minds of what a school looks like. Parents may not know how to work with their students on higher-level math or science or discuss new writers or events in social studies. Parent portals, school-home communication, and parent-teacher conferences often happen on the school's terms. With the demographic changes in the United States, teachers and parents may not speak the same language. With economic changes in the United States, even "professionals" may be working multiple jobs and have limited time to focus on a student during traditional hours. If parents work retail or utilize public transportation, going to school during "work hours" is a genuine hardship.

While you need to draw boundaries for your mental health as a teacher, you should also be flexible. Speak with your supervisor if you need to stay late, meet a parent on the weekend, or do a home visit. Work with professionals within your district or other agency to see if you need additional resources or information about how to work with a particular family. Your school should look at how the parent-home communications cycle honors your need as a teacher and the parents' needs to support you. Parents may need resources as well. How to work with children is complex and may require the intervention of medical or other professionals.

Utilize digital resources to help parents and students at home. In the same light, be aware of students and families who may not have the means or know-how to use technology or access the internet. You can work with your school and social services to help them get access.

Additionally, work with other teachers to create a series of virtual resources for parents to work with their child at home - not just on academic homework, but on creativity, citizenship, and communications. As family dynamics change, parents may seek resources from you. If you don't know, ask resources in your school for help.

You may also want access to parents' information on reducing electronic device usage. Social media creates additional and heightened concerns for parents, almost all of whom grew up (currently, give it five to seven years) without smartphones or social media. In years past, limiting screen time meant keeping children from hours of television consumption. Now, smartphones, tablets, and computers have monopolized and changed electro-neurons in people's brains (Carr. 2020).

Full disclosure, since I, Casey, am not a parent, but have been an educator for 20 years, and have seen friends and family members become parents, take what I say as an outside observer. When YOU become a parent, practice grace, and give yourself space to enjoy the journey. Parenting is the HARDEST job someone undertakes because you are now responsible for life besides your own. Be collaborative, communicative, and celebrate the wins.

Activity Putting Tip #11 Into Action: Working with Families

Directions: Identify some of the following questions you may have about working with families. Create the following chart as a guide for now and in the future. Share your thoughts with your PLN with the hashtag **#50TeacherTipsBook**.

My Questions	No Knowledge	Some Knowledge	A Fair Amount of Knowledge	A lot of Knowledge
Home school communication				
Grade questions				
Behavior questions				
Frequency of communications				
Your Own Question 1				
Your Own Question 2				

Tip 12: Asking Critical Questions: Are the Kids Safe? Does an Adult Care?

There are a lot of decisions teachers must make every minute (McGarr, 2021). Educational decision-making is emphasized heavily in teacher training. Teacher training teaches you to locate curriculum material and develop lessons based on English Language Arts standards. As a profession, we are still struggling with the actual implementation, as data-driven instruction, effective teaching practices, and supporting students, parents, and paraprofessionals are still a little bit of a black box and are often learned through practice rather than through study (Cuban, 2013).

Casey shares his Magic Three Question strategy.

Question 1: Are the kids safe?

It's a great question to start with. Physical safety is not the only factor to consider. While so many schools face threats of violence and potential gun violence, we must ensure students are alright by insiders, outsiders, and, frankly, a broken system. Recognizing students' and professionals', mental health needs are crucial and have grown in the past few years. Classrooms are influenced by the teacher, students, and how a culture of support and acceptance is created and implemented. With the growth of social media and personal electronic devices, cyberbullying is a critical and troublesome side effect. Teachers can start the year right by establishing a culture of collaboration. Even better, the class and the teacher can co-create the culture by establishing a few crucial rules and procedures. Adults and students co-create a positive climate by showing appreciation, creating opportunities for collaboration, and establishing a safe space to ensure internal or external violations are identified, recognized, reported, and remediated (Manolev et al., 2019) .

Question 2: Does an adult care?

Teaching is a service profession. Teaching is also an exhausting and intensive career. We care for other people's children. We create every formal learning opportunity. We are the gatekeepers of dreams. So as a classroom teacher, you must work with your team of co-teachers, other classroom teachers, the administration, teacher assistants, aides, and support staff to ensure that an adult cares about every student. This team approach can be created by establishing your reactions to students. You demonstrate support, and students appreciate your actions.

Demonstrating and modeling how to create a caring community through actions, words, and behaviors will carry far into the future. The children watch adults and can see when their behaviors do not match expectations. As an educator, a strengths-based approach and caring practices, which include communicating with the home, are essential to a profoundly impactful community of learners (Miller, 2021).

Question 3: Are they asking critical questions?

United States schools, since 2001, emphasized test-based knowledge (Ravitch, 2016). So-called reformers thought our schools were failing, teachers must be held accountable, and students needed to demonstrate mastery on high-stakes assessments. In reality, at best, testing has generated a lot of data to help schools make educated guesses or data-driven decisions. If done well, data can help students achieve by correctly diagnosing concerns with learning gaps. Data from tests could confirm that "gut feeling" many teachers have that a student is struggling with learning content or skills. However, we must be cautious, as testing and teaching to the test have overwhelmed a system that can encourage students to ask "Why?"

Casey shares, "My young niece and nephew (both under ten at the time of this writing) are constantly asking why, and how come, and what does this do, or mean? They take after their dad (my brother) and love to take apart complex items to see what processes make them tick." We love the curiosity that the children display. Yet, in American education, curiosity and engagement morphed into compliance when students reached middle and high school. So what happened? Often, asking critical questions or why becomes learning a rote set of facts or processes to "do school" (Washor & Mojkowski, 2014).

Activity Putting Tip #12 Into Action: Making the Magic Work With 3 Questions

Directions: Answer the following questions relating to the following. Share your thoughts with your PLN with the hashtag **#50TeacherTipsBook**.

- How will you ensure different types of safety?
- What are some ways you will show caring?
- What are some critical questions you want students to ask (not content-specific)?

Tip 13: Building Relationships Matters More Than Content

Start with sound teaching principles: develop a relationship with your students. Show them that you will help them deal with questions they raise because you value them individually and collectively. As a caring adult in the room, no matter what the standards or test results say, it would help if you focused on the most important thing: the student as a whole. Education in the United States is designed to change students. The system was designed for efficiency and compliance. United States education was designed to produce workers for an industrial system that is all about efficiency and control. Back-to-basics and accountability for learning are fundamentally rooted in a structural injustice: making poor and immigrant children fodder for machines and industries. Work with loyal workers who know how to do their jobs efficiently and effectively but never question their managers nor rebel against the low pay and poor working conditions of exploitation.

For the last 40 years, we have harassed teachers by holding them accountable for student achievement. Moreover, creativity and inventiveness are in short supply due to a compliance system that rivals the pre-World War II compliance model. Society wants compliant and creative children—all for the lowest possible public investment.

My wise people were raised on "Star Trek, Star Wars", "Harry Potter", and "Hunger Games". You are not a tribute to the system. You are the "only hope" or "the chosen one" or "the teacher who lived" or the volunteer as tribute who overthrew the system. To be an agent of change, start with the student: are they safe, do they know an adult cares, and ask critical questions? Take a genuine interest in and care for your students from the beginning. Don't get me wrong - some days will be more complex than others. On the first day of class, we ask our students about their interests, hobbies, extracurricular activities, pets, families, and future career or college plans.

Casey shares that at the end of week two, he asked his students about fears:

- What bothered students about the course?
- What worried them the most?

Many students wanted to know how to balance everything they expected in and out of school. They wanted to understand how they could attend school, do chores, participate in extracurriculars, and work. This was a lot for high school students. The pandemic means many older siblings are responsible for younger siblings during remote school days or staff shortage days. Students and adults are at breaking point. Rather than esoteric measures of minutia, we need caring people who can provide care.

Practice grace and give space as the year evolves. Don't penalize students for missing deadlines. Change difficult assignments into manageable explorations. Give students days to revise and edit their work as needed to demonstrate that they have learned. Model the genius hour, where your students can do whatever they want for one hour a week. Don't worry about content coverage. Focus instead on how well your students understand the opportunities that choice creates in the classroom. A deep dive into an exciting point can create dialogue, mentorship, and enjoyment beyond compliance engagement.

Through deliberate work, help students gain their abilities to see themselves as successful learners motivated by their interests, work, and goals by structuring and communicating success. We want students to remember more about how engaging and supportive the classroom was at the end of the year, not how drudgery reigned.

Activity Putting Tip #13 Into Action: Welcoming Classroom Environments

Directions: Answer the following prompts within the word cloud below. Each prompt can be used for any of the clouds. Share your thoughts with your PLN with the hashtag **#50TeacherTipsBook**. Identify the following:

- What can I, as a teacher, do to help my students feel welcome?
- What can I insist my students do to support each other?
- How can I work with the parents to ensure the students feel welcome?

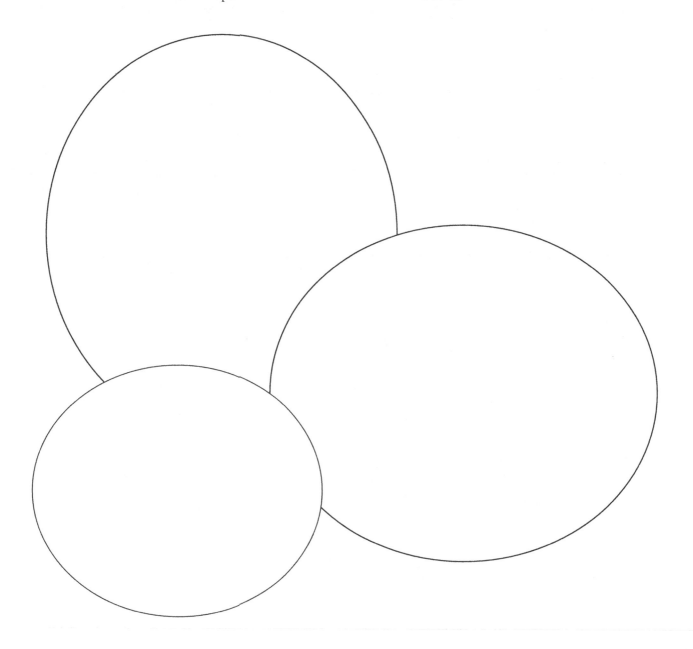

Tip 14: Special Education 101

According to the National Center for Education Statistics (2022), the number of students between ages 3 and 21 in the US who received special education-related services during the 202-2021 school year "under the Individuals with Disabilities Education Act (IDEA) was 7.2 million." IDEA covers 13 disabilities categories, including emotional, intellectual, and physical disabilities. Data shows a rise in students being diagnosed with disabilities since the 1970s. The most common disability category is learning disabilities, at 33% of all diagnoses. (National Center for Education Statistics, 2022). A student with a specific learning disability needs assistance understanding or using spoken and written language. It is possible that they need assistance with listening, speaking, reading, comprehension, writing, spelling, or calculating.

The National Center for Education Statistics (2022) goes on to share that students "with multiple disabilities, hearing impairments, orthopedic impairments, visual impairments, traumatic brain injuries, and deafblindness accounted for less than 2 percent of those served under IDEA."

All this to say, you will have students with different abilities and needs in your classroom. As teachers, we need to know how to adapt and differentiate instruction for our students to succeed and access our content. We know from our classes that we will have a wide range of learners in our class. While some typically develop, others may be gifted, and others may have a disability. We must start with accessibility in mind first, not as an afterthought. So when we plan a lesson, we need to support our students throughout our lesson. When lesson planning, think about these prompts:

- How will my students access the content I'm teaching?
- What content am I teaching during this lesson?
- What are the objectives of my lesson?
- How do I know my students understood the objectives?
- How will I differentiate what I'm teaching to my students?
- What accommodations or modifications are needed?
- Which universal design for learning strategies will I implement?
- How will I scaffold my lesson for learners?
- How will my students show what they know at the end of the lesson?

By thinking about accessibility first and how students will access the content, you can help your students get to the content. You are designing for all in mind when you do this. Dr. Sam shares that when she went to college, one of her professors told her never to look at the IEP before meeting the students. While she understands that the professor meant not to put judgements or limitations on a student before meeting them, it is essential to know what the students need to access the curriculum. Dr. Sam shares that her advice to new teachers would be to review the IEP for each student in your class. Jot down important dates associated with the IEP, accommodations, modifications, services needed and when the student receives services, and other important information about the student. Essentially you are creating a quick sheet that covers essential topics found in the IEP. However, don't let yourself automatically place limitations or expectations on the student before meeting them. Get to know the student as an individual who needs support to access the curriculum and content. Also, feel free to reach out to the previous teacher or case manager for additional ways to support the student.

Activity Putting Tip #14 Into Action: One Sheet

Directions: Create a one-sheet for each student on your roster with an IEP. This way, you have an easy reference for essential information found in the IEP document. Share your thoughts with your PLN with the hashtag **#50TeacherTipsBook**.

Student initials	
Strengths	
Areas of need	
IEP meeting date	
IEP revision date	
IEP implementation dates	
Special education-related services (and schedule of services)	Monday Tuesday Wednesday Thursday Friday
Accommodations	
Modifications	
Notes	

Tip 15 - Navigating 504, IEP, and SST Meetings

You must attend Student Study Team, 504, and Individual Education Plan (IEP) meetings throughout the year. All these meetings are related to supporting students who may need additional support or may have a documented disability. Before attending these meetings, you will receive students at the beginning of the year where disabilities and additional support may be documented. Ultimately, this is a big part of the teaching duties you will have to navigate - sometimes even the most difficult. Before jumping into how to prepare and navigate these various meetings, let's first define what each stands for.

First, Student Study Team meetings (SST) are opportunities for stakeholders and server providers of the student to evaluate student progress if a student falls behind before a referral may be given for further assessment to determine if a disability manifests. A 504 meeting throughout this tip refers to Section 504 is part of the Rehabilitation Act of 1973, which states any entity or organization that receives financial funding must ensure all persons with disabilities are not discriminated against relating to goods or services and aspects of employment. Various services and accommodations must be given to students who qualify for these services. Similar to 504 meetings, IEP meetings relate to the Individuals with Disabilities Act, which requires services to be provided by schools to students who fall under various disabilities that may impact their participation within the general education curriculum.

There may be students in your class who may not have any documented support or disability but begin to appear to fall behind. Thus, part of our responsibilities as a teacher is to support all students and identify students who may need additional support. As a result, there are several meetings teachers are required to prepare for and participate in throughout the year to ensure the school support team is working towards meeting the student where they are at and amplifying their strengths.

Preparing for Meetings

To prepare for these meetings, we must collect formative and summative data and qualitative data in the form of observations. Formative data includes data recently collected on the student, in addition to work samples produced over the weeks leading up to the meeting. Additionally, summative data from school/district and state assessments can be collected and provided. Last, qualitative observations were collected about the student's behavior, executive functioning, social interactions, and emotional well-being. Various stakeholders, including the student's teacher, collect this information. Sometimes meetings are held before families are brought into meetings to evaluate the data further. It ultimately will depend on the circumstance. Ultimately, a written report and data sheets should be developed and provided to the family along with a plan at least 24 hours before the meeting (regardless of meeting type).

Don't worry. As mentioned before, this should not all fall under a teacher's responsibility. Rather, it should be a collaborative effort, including school site admin. Stakeholders may include the general education teacher, school psychologist, social worker, speech pathologist, and Special Education teacher. It may even include educators at the district office, including Assistive Technology, Head of Special Education, or Program Specialist. If stakeholders are involved, communicate with them, provide them with the information they may need, and know that it's a team effort. The team effort will make or break the case. Not you, the teacher of the student.

Student Study Team Meetings (SST Meetings)

Student Study Team meetings allow a team of stakeholders to meet to evaluate if a student needs further support, interventions, and possibly even more assessment. Generally, the teacher monitors their executive functions, behaviorally or socially emotionally, in their class before making a determination of whether they need to refer the student to the SST.. Each school has a process of referral, which may include a survey or communication form. After the referral and data to support the referral have been provided, a meeting is scheduled, and the student's family is invited. The meeting involves reviewing student progress, discussing interventions, and ultimately determining whether more assessments must occur to determine if a disability manifests itself. SST meetings and procedures differ at various schools and states. As a result, consult your principal, psychologists, and Special

Education teachers on the procedures for initiating an SST meeting on your campus.

504 and IEP Meetings

504 and IEP meetings may require more preparation beforehand because a student's IEP or 504 is a legal document that legally bind service providers, including teachers who provide some of those services, to support the student in their learning beyond what's offered to all students in the general education curriculum. By law, all service providers must provide input and be a stakeholder in developing the education plans that manifest themselves as services for the student to meet them where they are at depending on their individual needs.

To prepare for the meetings and the documentation that concurrently goes with each meeting, be sure you are constantly collecting data and keeping the students' and work samples within a digital folder. The Special Education teacher may provide data sheets or forms for specific goals. A data-sheet can be completed by physically writing on it and uploading the document or through a digital survey. Academic goals can be tied to various types of assessments. Using tools like adaptive EdTech like iReady provides assessments and lessons geared towards meeting the students where they are academic, providing a more straightforward mechanism for you to collect your data. Beyond the data collection, you will be asked to write down qualitative notes relating to their academics, social-emotional well-being, behavior, and executive functioning that may also be utilized by the IEP team and Special Education case manager in the draft of the IEP. Therefore, an organization is critical, and preparation beforehand is necessary so all the information can be consolidated and given to all the stakeholders and service providers when needed.

Beyond preparation, communication before, during, and after the meeting is essential to building and maintaining relationships with the student and their family. 504 and IEP meetings can be contentious, as well as very positive. As a result, in terms of communication, focus on strength-based communication, starting with outlining a strength and how that strength can be used to help overcome and improve an area of improvement of the student. Communication also relates to the team of educators at that IEP or 504 meetings. A solid message and game plan are essential to staying on message. This is a team effort, but you have the opportunity to help cultivate that message since you work with that student directly.

Conclusion and More Tips and Tricks to Consider

When you arrive on a new campus, always ask about how each of these three meetings is conducted at your school site and the procedures for preparing and being an active team member. Additionally, meet various service providers and stakeholders as they are essential to know as resources to help support you if you see a student struggling. They are vital teammates to help you identify, provide documentation and interventions, and initiate further discussions. Further, they will help you provide support and services for students with the scaffolds outlined in their IEP and 504 plans. Beyond what was discussed in this tip, several important points were summarized below as critical strategies to help you prepare and navigate these meetings.

- Use a Google Drive or OneDrive with folders dedicated to student IEPs and 504, student data, student work, and meeting logs/notes.
- Use Google Forms, Microsoft Forms, or SurveyMonkey to collect student data for stakeholders' SST, 504, and IEP meetings. Or, as a general education teacher, be sure to **ALWAYS** complete IEP Goal or Present Level data forms.
- Your student information system and learning management system are your best friends. Use the data found in each to help you and your team collect student data and work samples for upcoming meetings.
- Create folders in your email to document communication. Always document. Whether for ANY student, family, and service provider communication or students you will have an IEP, SST, or 504 meeting, always document and save your emails in an organized manner.

Activity Putting Tip #15 Into Action: Preparing for SST, 504, and IEP Meetings

Directions: Create a workflow of procedures you will need to ensure you are prepared for these meetings. Write your list of procedures below in the graphic organizer. Share your thoughts with your PLN with the hashtag **#50TeacherTipsBook**.

List of Procedures to Prepare for SST, 504, and IEP Meetings

Tip 16: Multilingual Learners - All Students Are Language Learners

All students are language learners. Students may be learning their first language, second, third, or even fourth language. Regardless of the content and skills you are teaching, new uses of language will be taught and learned by your students. New vocabulary and how they use it in the context of the content and skills they are taught are fundamental to putting their new knowledge and skills to practice. Thus, within our lessons, we must design them with language supports and differentiations so that our language learning students can pick can pick up the new language you are teaching them so they can put it to practice. You will see how we can create language supports and differentiations that amplify what you are doing to support multilingual learners in your classroom. We will also discuss how retrieval practice and repetition are essential for students to build their vocabulary necessary for them to build the skills and content you are teaching them in your class.

Create Language Supports and Differentiations Built into Your Lessons

Try to have a listening, speaking, writing, and creation component for each of your lessons. This satisfies the elements of the Universal Design for Learning (UDL) and is also advantageous to multilingual learners. Within each of these elements discussed, you can have various mechanisms to provide opportunities for your multilingual learners to access the lesson and curriculum. For example, you can teach your students to use Google Translate, which is embedded in Docs, a Google Chrome browser extension, and a web-based website. Additionally, you can share with students how to use voice typing. It is found underneath the "Tools" button on the main interface of Docs, which can be used to help students dictate their writing. There are other tools such as Mote, Pear Deck, Nearpod, Flip, and Padlet where you can provide recorded audio and videos where you can front load content and provide it in another form of multimedia outside of the text.

Besides adding multidimensional support from tools, you can also focus on various strategies. One strategy you can implement along with these supports is Think, Write, Pair, and Share. Students first are introduced to a prompt where they are required to think about it before writing or solving a problem. The prompt can include a graphic, audio recording, video, and text, which can be integrated directly into a slideshow where it is displayed. Then, students are asked to write or solve the prompt at hand. It can be done on paper or with an interactive EdTech tool. Teachers with this opportunity can see each of their students' answers in real-time, which can help them determine who needs additional support. After completing writing and problem solving, students are prompted to share their answers with a classmate aloud. Sentence frames can be provided to support them in that process, as well as directions asking students to be ready to explain their partner's response before discussing their response with the class. The last and final step is students are asked to share what they have written or discuss the problem they have solved and explain their reasoning. As illustrated through this strategy, students are required to think, problem solve, write, communicate, and collaborate. These skills are transferable in the content and skills you are teaching them and in language.

Retrieval Practice and Using Academic Discourse to Practice Builds Language Skills

Retrieval practice relates to using recall to short-term memory to engrain it into long-term memory further. The goal is to take our working and short-term memories and move them into our long-term memories. Flashcards, braindumps, practice opportunities, summaries, and reflections are strategies that help with this. These strategies are all content and skill agnostic (they can be used teaching any content area or skill) and can be utilized to help students build vocabulary. To further amplify these strategies, provide opportunities for collaborative student conversations. For example, students can practice flashcards together and be asked to use the term in a sentence when they quiz each other.

Another example is having students outline each element of their summary, brain dump, or reflection. Reading is not enough. Instead, it may be provided by their teacher to dissect why each student decided to add the content and thoughts to their finished work product.

Additionally, exercises such as gallery walks and digital gallery walks allow students to rotate and discuss their thoughts regarding the work they have created with multiple students.

We Live in a World of Multilingualism

We have the most support and tools available to support our students in becoming multilingual learners. If your classroom has digital tools available, you can add several supports directly to each task your students complete. However, as discussed above, students can build their vocabulary and speaking skills while problem-solving by sequencing strategies that are UDL friendly, such as Think, Write, Pair, and Share. We recommend thinking of similar strategies in addition to incorporating the language supports. Harvard Project Zero Thinking Routines are a great place to find many thinking routines to help build content knowledge and skills while building language skill sets.

Activity Putting Tip #16 Into Action: Implementing Supports and Strategies for a Multilingual Classroom

Directions: How do you plan on using differentiated language supports and retrieval practice in your class to support and build multilingualism? Additionally, consider what EdTech tools you can integrate with these strategies to amplify student learning further. Complete the following table by brainstorming how you can integrate these various strategies into your classroom instruction. Share your thoughts with your PLN with the hashtag **#50TeacherTipsBook**.

Differentiated Language Supports	Retrieval Practice	EdTech Tools

Critical Conversation One: Mental Health, Self-Harm, and Suicide Prevention

Trigger warning This Critical Conversation discusses the topic of suicide and self-harm among students. Please read this section in a safe space and have resources ready. The National Suicide Hotline is 800-273-8255, and you can also find helpful information on their website at: https://suicidepreventionlifeline.org/

A teacher's job does not start and end at content. We are tasked with the enormous responsibility of educating students while understanding, meeting and supporting the needs that they bring into the classroom. This includes the vital topic of mental health.

Most teachers are not mental health experts. However, we are "first responders" to our student's mental health and well-being. Students often reach out to teachers first to express self-harm and suicide ideation issues. The importance cannot be understated, as we may be their first and, if ignored, the last contact.

The statistics are staggering. Approximately 17% of teens have engaged in self-harm (Gillies et al., 2018), with the numbers steadily rising. These numbers rise exponentially for students of marginalized communities. 14.24 children per 100,000 from ages 15-24 commit suicide (afsp.org, 2020). The numbers show that in any given year, you are likely to have students in your classroom who have engaged in self-harm and have thoughts about suicide.

The following conversation is a dialogue with the four authors of this book on the topic of student mental health, self-harm, and suicide. We have all been involved in situations of this nature, though it has never been easy for any of us to discuss or work through. We did our best to be genuine and authentic with the conversation.

One important note before you dive into the conversation with us: our role in suicide prevention is to provide spaces where students can express their needs to us to pair them with the appropriate resources. We are often not the resource they need. We are the trusted adults in their lives, though. Use that trust and be mindful of how students express themselves to ensure they receive the proper guidance and resources to prevent self-injury.

Kevin: One of the essential things in schools is mental health, which impacts every level of education. It impacts student success, their wellness, their joy, and their ability to graduate and go to better things, and it even impacts their lives, so what we're talking about today is how to support students. What should we do as teachers, and what do we do if things escalate, like suicide ideation or suicide attempts? As teachers, we've all been in certain situations where we've talked to students. How do you guys recognize when a student might need some intervention, and how do you tell how serious the intervention needs to be or other strategies to identify those situations?

Sam: I'd like to jump in and start with the importance of getting rid of the stigma of mental health issues in the classroom and just having it be a theme that we talk about, checking in on our students, making it every day in our classroom that we check in with their students, no matter what grade or subject that you're teaching. Just checking in with them, not about coursework, but checking in with them as human beings, knowing that your course is not the main focus of their life, and that's okay. Just checking in with them regularly to see how they're doing, how you can support them, and what they are excited about coming up. What are they struggling with? How can you help, be supportive and serve your students? I think, first and foremost, avoiding the stigma of mental health and making mental health a priority in the classroom.

Matt: I like to do social and emotional learning at the beginning and end of each class. For example, I like to use interactive slides. I like having students circle how they're feeling and maybe describe how they're feeling or an experience or a social story-type concept. Depending on the age of students we're working with, those types of opportunities at the beginning and the end of class allow you to get a vibe of how the whole class may be doing. As well as providing that opportunity for that student to reflect and build their emotional intelligence.

Casey: All excellent points, and the only one I'd like to add, is to modify a quote I heard from a teacher I know: "Worry about yourself too." I think it's essential that we all start by saying the mental health crisis begins with the adults because we are so engaged in day-to-day caring that we are often experiencing massive horrible amounts of burnout. It's a systematic flaw that depends on teachers volunteering and caring to supply our students' needs emotionally. One essential piece of advice I can give besides teachers healing themselves first is to take a step back. If you look at the expectations placed upon our career over the past 20 years, they're far exceeding what any person can do alone. Make sure you work in teams and also make sure that you tell students growth is the goal, perfection is the enemy, and I think that what we all need to keep in mind is if we practice grace, we practice self-forgiveness. We practice coaching so that we're going to make it, but we first have to recognize it starts with your state.

Kevin: Those are all great points. Looking at teachers, you know that modeling is a crucial part of any instruction. So teachers should model good self-health routines. Making sure that you're managing your emotional well-being is an important step. Matt and Sam, great suggestions for having those opportunities to reflect with and check in with all of your students regularly. That consistency is significant. Along with that, what strategies do you use to support their well-being within a lesson? We often talk about SEL as a side thing, and when we talk about mental health, it's the beginning or the end of class. But I know I've had plenty of moments where students were having breakdowns and crying during the lesson. What do you do to counsel students and help them individually or as a group? How do you deal with that versus your instructional time?

Casey: Kevin, you're starting with something that I think, especially many new teachers, aren't sure how to start with, which is giving students space and helping them feel comfortable talking to you because it may not be related to your math lesson. It may be related to a more significant issue that's going on in the world, or, in your opinion, it may be a minor issue, but to the students, it's a massive issue at the moment.

I think the second most important strategy that we have is that we need to treat our students with the same level of humanism that we want ourselves to be treated with. When I was teaching, I allowed them to excuse themselves from taking a long walk to a long bathroom or a long water fountain break because sometimes you need that. We go into the car and confess to our steering wheel how bad the day was. Sometimes students need to find a safe place.

I think the third area is to create better expectations for our students. They need to know what they're expected to do. Rubrics help, as well as game plans and scaffolding, so it doesn't feel overwhelming. It is a huge win if they know how to complete the tasks in an organized fashion. They will be able to identify how to get those small wins. Finally, recognizing those small wins, Kevin is so critical. You have to support them along the way.

Matt: I love how you talk about giving your students space to go and walk out of the classroom and get a drink of water. Then possibly when they come back, if it's more like independent group activities, you can essentially go and have a short check-in conversation with them. I've also used my learning management system to directly provide all of our schools' mental health and community resources on the front page. There are links for them to contact any counselor, social worker, or whoever the school has a relationship with, which is essential. It stresses to you that, hey, these resources are there. Then, one thing regarding modeling it yourself, you don't have to say everything about your personal life but discuss how you're navigating certain situations. For example, how you're holding multiple hats or taking care of yourself. Are you going to the gym or maybe even being open about your mental health, saying that you may be having a tough day right now? I've enjoyed talking to someone in the past, and that's helped me in my personal growth, so those are some things you can think about as being open and providing those resources for your students.

Sam: I would say the biggest thing that helps support students with their mental health is grace over grades, not being so strict that they have to get it done by Sunday at midnight, or else you'll lose two points. Something's going on in their life. Be gracious and treat people well like Casey was sharing.

Be gracious with students because they will come back to help you. If you put good karma out, it will come back. Being gracious with your students doesn't come right away. You have to build those relationships with them and connect with them, so they can share something going on in their personal life. They may have just broken up with their boyfriend, which might seem insignificant to us, but it's very much their world. I think reaching them where they are and showing them grace, whether giving them an extra day or allowing them to turn in what they have so far, and I'll give them feedback on that, and we'll work on that together. Or, instead of taking this test right now, how about we do something else? You can come in during office hours, and we can do an oral exam.

Maybe it's something severe like maybe there's a death in the family or something that's affecting them. Maybe it's just a 10-point assignment, just dropping that assignment for them and moving on. Instead of doing the assignment, we're just going to drop that. Add that to your total points, and that'll be okay. They will still learn without that assignment. Being gracious over greed and not being so point-oriented, instead being person-oriented.

Kevin: The trends I'm hearing so far are humanizing education and providing resources. One of the hardest things new teachers will have to deal with is determining when something needs to be escalated to help outside your classroom. As teachers, we always want to be very helpful, and we want to be trusted adults in their life. Still, when a student comes up to you with an issue that makes you a mandatory reporter and puts you in the shoes where you need to gather that outside help and bring resources in for that student, it can be challenging to find that boundary. What's the difference between them telling you something important to them verse something that may be life-threatening or might be suicide ideation that requires you to be a mandatory reporter and take it to that next step?

I'd like to hear your thoughts on where you determine that line of *I can handle this in my classroom, versus I need to get this person to a school counselor, and we need to escalate the situation beyond what I can do in my classroom.* Remember that one of the most challenging parts of this is the popularity of self-deprecating humor. Students make fun of themselves and always say negative things about themselves. Is it a joke or not? How do we determine those issues that might be more serious?

Sam: I want to go back to the case you mentioned initially. Using that team approach, if it's something you can feel in your gut like, *oh, we need to report this, or I need to get help with this, I am not a certified counselor. Let's get some help here.* Sometimes if a student comes to my office feeling overwhelmed or upset, I suggest them taking a break, take a breath, and walk down to the counseling center. Let's go together, and I can help to support them. I'm not a certified counselor. I'm a certified teacher. I can help. I can listen.

But, I think going to a counselor or a guidance counselor or therapist will be more helpful for you to help support you in this. Let them know that I'm here, I hear you, and I want to help you get support, picking that team approach.

Casey: I want you to be mad at me for the rest of your life. Because you're angry at me rather than having to go to your funeral, and I think that having experienced suicide, you will never forgive yourself if you don't do something. I would rather you be mad at me for the rest of your life than have to attend your funeral.

Matt: I love the team approach, building a relationship with the school psychologist, the social worker, the education specialist, the assistant principal, and the principal. Any support staff that may help you navigate any crisis is massive because each brings expertise. They bring their relationship, possibly with the student. Also, having some relationship with the family is incredibly important, not only for yourself, hopefully, but for the school community, especially if they've been navigating those difficult circumstances. It's just harnessing those connections and notifying that team of individuals once something is up and where that needs to have attention drawn.

Kevin: I want to add that whenever I was trying to determine if something needed further assistance, I was always looking for keywords that either dealt with self-harm or keywords that talked about somebody deserving something terrible that's happened to them. When I heard something like that, it gave me a clue that there might be something more significant going on than just sadness about an issue, but they might be considering self-harm.

You know the context of that student if you're building relationships. You know them well and understand what kind of language they're using and if they're actively seeking you out or if they're hiding away. They're looking for a way to get that help before it's too late, so when you have students coming up to your desk, you have to take it seriously no matter what words they're saying.

So now, to take that one step further, I've been in the terrible circumstance of students who have self-harmed and students who have committed suicide. They were the most challenging times in my teaching career. Many of us have been through moments like that, either with our students or students in the community or neighboring communities, impacting us as educators. Still, as teachers, we also have to focus on what's happening with our other students when something like that happens. When there is an attempt or a suicide in your community, what can you do to support the students in your classroom who probably knew that student or grew up with them? What can we do as educators to support students in those moments?

Casey: The first part of understanding what to do to support students in the wake of a tragedy stems from a work that I read called Teaching the Day After by Dunn from the Columbia Teachers College. In the book, Professor Dunn identifies a few steps that teachers need to take, and the first one is to allow students the opportunity and space to identify where they are. Some of your classes may be 100% impacted by the event, some may only be slightly impacted, and others may not. You as the teacher need to work with your team at the school to identify how and why, and where to provide your students with the most critical support, which include the following: are they safe, do they know an adult cares, and do they know how to access help? It's okay to say that I don't know how to deal with this, and I'm not sure what to do. I'm grieving with everyone, too.

It would help if you also took an opportunity to allow students to have conflicting emotions. While this may be a huge issue, they may also be experiencing other emotions simultaneously because of other events in their lives and will be conflicted. While we are trained as pedagogues, content providers, and learning providers, we are not mental health counselors. As educators, we are first aid only and must be sure to hand off the more severe cases successfully. Just like if somebody is injured at an event, I can help them by getting a Band-Aid on them, but I might need an EMT to do something more invasive.

As a teacher, I need to know my boundaries and how to help my students by saying I don't know what I don't know, but I'm with you on this journey.

Matt: The analogy of the EMT first responder is significant when thinking about these types of situations that occur. As the school community provides opportunities for students to get those resources to navigate their emotions, it's good to drop whatever you're doing and give them the opportunity if they have counselors on site. If there are support animals, have them go to those. Drop everything that you're doing. It's not about learning the content toward a skill at this point. It's about providing that team for your students to navigate how they're feeling, to receive the support, and then hopefully come back together as a class community and the school community.

Kevin: I know this is a complicated topic. It's tough for us to talk about. I'm sure it's going to be tough for anybody who's reading this. To even conceptualize what these moments are like, we never want to think about these moments, but at the same time, we don't want any teacher to feel unprepared when a moment like this happens. We have gone through it in many ways, and have experienced this myself. I was much like Casey. I don't know how to help you, but I can grieve with you. I can be here with you in moments of tragedy, and this isn't related to suicide. Still, any traumatic issue that happens within the Community or the school, just being present allows you to feel feelings with the students and go through the process with them.

You can be honest and point them to outside resources and say look, I'm not the professional for this thing. I'm not the person that can tell you what the next steps are, what to do, or how to grieve appropriately. Still, I can support you by being with you and going through this process together.

Just like we differentiate our instruction, I've learned that people have differentiated needs when they deal with trauma. Some people want to work and try to get their minds off it, while others can't open a book and think about work. As a teacher, it's essential to provide all of that range so that your students can cope in the way that's going to be most effective for them. Anytime a tragedy struck when I was teaching, that was an important step. I would say, "Hey, if you want some things you can work on, here's some stuff on the side of the whiteboard. It's buried in that corner, you don't even have to look at it, but it's there if you want it."

We could do that if they just wanted to sit and talk and have some dialogue. If they want some quiet time to read to themselves, listen to music, or cope in that way, that's okay, too. You're a space provider so find suitable spaces to help your students. Continue pairing them with the resources and professionals who will be able to assist them further. We must take all those steps together so that students have places to go and ways to get through probably one of the most challenging times of their life.

Final Thoughts - Critical Conversation #1

Perhaps Casey said it best when describing teachers as first responders. When it comes to suicide ideation and self-harm, teachers are often the first to know or even have a suspicion of it. This does not make us the most equipped to handle and deescalate the situation, but it does make us the nearest, trusted adults. Therefore, it is critical to pair students with appropriate resources.

Suicide prevention is a team effort. Make sure that you know your team within the school and your resources outside of the school. Have contacts ready and plan discreetly when you need room coverage to escort a student to a counselor. Know your mandatory reporting process and requirements. Strong communication in this area can be a life-or-death matter.

SECTION 2: WHEN THE GOING GETS TOUGH

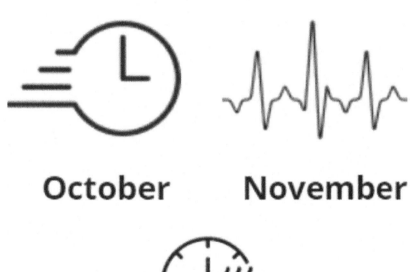

October   November

December

"When the going gets tough, take a coffee break." - Stephen Hawking

Section 2: When the Going Gets Tough

Getting ready for school was the focus of our previous section. Now that the tires have hit the road, you feel like they have left a trail behind. After the initial "rush" and adrenaline of the school year's beginning, you begin to see the routine, the weather, the first marking period, the special events, and the demands of committees or extracurriculars. Even worse, this is the season when the graduate school semester becomes...difficult for those in classes since the first assignments are typically due when the five-week reports are due. This part of the year is tricky because you begin to consume more caffeine and sleep less. Stop.

- Eat a healthy diet
- Drink water for your health.
- Give yourself one day a week where you stop grading everything and allow students the joy of peer feedback. Alright? Breath in….and out. Ok, Zen feelings.

Tips and Strategy Entries 17-27

Tip 17: Setting Boundaries With Your Time

We must protect our time as educators, especially as new teachers. This is a lesson that we wish we knew as new teachers and practiced earlier in our careers. Sam shares that when she began teaching, she went to school an hour early and stayed two or three hours after contract time, five days a week. This was unsustainable, and she quickly found herself overwhelmed with all that she needed to do. As new teachers, it's a hard pill to swallow because we want to do all the things. We understand that it's hard to say no as a new teacher. But, it's essential to know that we must protect our time. You will be asked to do many things as a new teacher, including activities and commitments outside your contract hours. You should set boundaries with your time and commitments. As a new teacher, please know that you. don't have to say yes to everything. Know that you can say "no" to opportunities. You don't have to join every committee or volunteer for every opportunity. Consider what you are saying yes to before you say yes. Take a step back to reflect and say, "I'll think about this opportunity and get back to you tomorrow morning." By taking a step back, you'll be able to assess a situation. Think about the pros and cons of this decision and the impact it will have on your life. Some questions to reflect upon:

- Is this a short or long-term commitment? Is this something you need to do this week or month?
- If this is a committee, how often does the committee meet? When? Where? How long are the meetings?
- If it's long, will you be just as excited as you are now about it in a few months or when the activity is during the year?
- Consider the time of the year this opportunity is in - during the beginning of the year or the end. Is it during the testing time? When is it during the week?
- Will you need time to work on it outside of the classroom? If so, how much time? Do you have time for this opportunity?
- Do you have the time to commit to participating to the best of your ability?
- How does this opportunity fit with your stage of life and career goals?

You don't have to bring work home every day. Consider this: your to-do list and work will still be there in the morning when you return. This is why it's essential to go back to our first tip - do less with more and prioritize your tasks. Bringing homework every night and weekend doesn't make you a better teacher. What makes you a better teacher is being efficient in your work.

Don't stay late every day. You can leave at your contract time. Find a partner who holds you accountable to leave on time. Make one day a week that you are leaving on contract time and see if you can increase that to 3 (or more) days. Additionally, feel free to take days off for your mental health. Ultimately, setting boundaries around your time is essential to taking care of yourself. After school hours, you don't need to check your email. You do not have to have your work email on your phone. Establish boundaries for when you check and respond to emails. In doing so, you will consider your mental health. It's okay to disconnect from school when you aren't there so you can focus on yourself.

It's easy to say yes. But as a new teacher, you must protect your time and well-being. As a new teacher, it is hard to say "no" or decline an offer, but if you set firm boundaries around your time, you can find more time for yourself. You can invest in others when you have more time for yourself.

Activity Putting Tip #17 Into Action: Setting Boundaries You Can Stick To

Directions: Consider the tips mentioned above to protect your time as a new teacher. Jot down in the space below how you will set boundaries for yourself. Share your thoughts with your PLN with the hashtag **#50TeacherTipsBook**.

Tip 18: Seeking Strengths - Asset-Based Pedagogy

Focusing on deficits is becoming increasingly evident in the school system. At a young age, students are shown what they don't know, asked why they don't know it, then given standardized tests to measure their performance against state standards. All the standards that drive their learning are based on skills they must master or else.

Deficits don't stop there for many students. Every teacher they meet has expectations, which may be difficult for that child to meet. It is epitomized in the language we hear from teachers every day. "Why can't you sit in your chair?" or "How are you not getting this formula? This is simple. You need to know how to do this." You can probably think of plenty of other phrases you have heard as a student or by observing other classes.

The "fun" doesn't stop at school. Students go home to a completely different set of expectations, with families or caretakers who may have different priorities that highlight even more deficits. Some students may not have to deal with their perceived shortcomings at every turn, but countless students do.

It can be challenging to reverse this viewpoint as an educator. After all, you are also under pressure. It is your job to bring students' standards up to par and to correct their deficiencies. It may seem counterintuitive to focus less on deficiencies when trying to raise student scores and enhance their progress.

However, a better method exists for bringing students to a higher level. The asset-based pedagogy enables teachers to address deficits but in a way that honors and respects students. This does not mean you ignore their knowledge gaps or fail to teach them challenging information. Instead, it is about fostering the best efforts of your students while putting yourself in the role of a co-learner.

Honoring and valuing our students' strengths validates their experience as students. In contrast, when we ignore the strengths and experiences of our students to focus on the coursework, we invalidate them. Consider the impact on students who do not learn, think, or express themselves traditionally or expectedly. Depending on the teacher's response, they may feel heard, represented, consequential, ignored, unappreciated, or stupid. Focusing on deficits can only harm your progress when creating a positive learning environment.

There are many ways to recognize your students' contributions to the classroom. Your strategies should be authentic and relevant to the curriculum and standards you are addressing. While it is a complex field, there are straightforward ways to begin to shift to an asset-based pedagogy. It begins with a commitment. Your commitment to understanding the experiences and strengths your students bring to the classroom will set you on the right path. Think about the timing and structure of a typical lesson.

- Is there an opportunity for students to connect the material to their knowledge?
- Have they had a chance to give input on what they are learning, why, and how?
- Is anyone's voice or experience being ignored in your classroom because they do not express themselves in the way you prefer?

With an assets-based approach, you don't have to forget everything you know as a teacher or sacrifice your planned work. You must be a co-learner, willing to let students lead and share their experiences. Positive evaluation of their narratives and experiences will validate that they are students worthy of respect and esteem. By seeing themselves in that light, students are more likely to build upon their strengths, be confident in the classroom, and put forth their best effort to further their learning.

College courses and books are dedicated to analyzing and discussing this topic. Keep researching and growing in this field. The most important thing is to get started. Find out how different experiences can be enriching. Look for each student's strengths and qualities.

Activity Putting Tip #18 Into Action: Being a Strength Seeker

Directions: Let's start honoring your students and valuing their talents. Jot down the name of each student in your class. Next to their name, write down 3-5 areas of strength. If you can't immediately write down a response, schedule a 5-minute sit down with that student and find out. Share your thoughts with your PLN with the hashtag **#50TeacherTipsBook**.

Student Name	Areas of Strength and Talent	Strategies to Showcase the Strength in the Classroom/Lesson

Tip 19: Practicing I Do, We Do, and You Do and Gradual Release

The gradual release is one of the best strategies for teaching students. Essentially, it is to demonstrate how to perform a task and allow the students to complete it more independently as time passes. In this way, students can learn the information or skills they need to accomplish a task, allowing them to complete the task independently. Gradual release can be implemented in your classroom through the I Do, We Do, and You Do strategy. It allows the teacher to model the task and then allows students to collaborate independently before completing the final task. In addition to serving as a scaffold, it allows students to complete a task more independently once provided with this instructional sequence.

Our goal is to demonstrate and illustrate the instructional sequence of this strategy. In addition, we want to demonstrate how it is a strategy that can be used in any classroom setting. We want to show you its ease of use as a go-to strategy that can amplify your instruction and student learning.

To conduct the instructional sequence of *I Do, We Do, and You Do*, we begin by modeling and instructing directly. Modeling and direct instruction involve demonstrating how to do or complete a task or skill and discussing how it can be done. Modeling can be done using a shared screen, video, document camera, whiteboard, or even acting out a task or skill you would like your students to learn. Try to keep your modeling and direct instruction short, with five minutes being the maximum time you want to spend modeling and providing direct instruction.

The next step is determining a collaborative task for students to participate in. Whether a small group of three to four or a pair of two students, this collaborative task takes what you've modeled and provided direct instruction and puts it into students' hands. For example, say you have demonstrated how to solve a particular type of math problem. You illustrated each step and modeled how to complete and solve the problem. Now, the students will collaborate to solve a similar type of problem. This can be done for essentially any content. During the collaborative time, set routines and protocols for students to follow. These can include roles in a group, the number of times students are given, and appropriate ways of how students can collaborate. Last, it is good to note how much support you as the teacher will play during this collaborative time that students work together. Depending on the complexity of the task will help you determine how much support you will need to provide. This support may include check-ins or stopping the entire class from providing more modeling and direct instruction.

The final step is for students to complete a similar task independently. They have had exposure through modeling, direct instruction, and practice working together in a group collaboration. Now, it's time for the student to try it on their own with little support from the teacher.

I Do, We Do, and You Do strategy for the gradual release can be conducted essentially in any classroom setting. Breakout rooms and a slideshow are utilized within an online setting instead of pairs or groups at tables, which share the task for students to complete. A teacher can share their screen and model and provide direct instruction throughout the modeling and direct instruction within an online setting. Through these three changes of modalities of how the strategy is facilitated, the sequence of the strategy does not change. Besides breakout rooms, slides can be employed in any interactive way by students or groups whereby a teacher can see the individual student and group's progress throughout the various stages of the strategy. For example, by deploying a slideshow using Pear Deck or Nearpod, a teacher can see exactly what students write down or draw on their slides in real-time. To further note, this can also be done in person. Seeing students work in real-time allows for formative feedback to be given throughout the strategy as students are gradually released to become more independent in completing the task and problem at hand.

Gradual release through the *I Do, We Do, and You Do* strategy is a powerful strategy that can be done in any classroom setting. Also, it allows students to process information in many different ways, cooperate with peer(s), and solve a problem independently over time. Ultimately, we want our students to be able to solve the tasks and problems they encounter in life. Gradual release in school demonstrates how they can do this as a lifelong learner; especially in a world where so much of what we can learn can be reviewed at any time through video. Therefore, it is a practical and applicable strategy that makes a massive difference in student learning.

Activity Putting Tip #19 Into Action Activity: Agree, Mini-Lesson, & Reflect

Directions: What areas do you agree with after reading this tip? Then, in the second box, create a short mini-lesson outline using gradual release. Third, reflect upon how your mini-lesson went using this strategy. Share your thoughts with your PLN with the hashtag **#50TeacherTipsBook**.

Agree

Mini-Lesson

Reflect

Tip 20: Planning for Interdisciplinary Units

Quality and effective instruction starts with good planning and the ability to pivot when necessary. One of the hallmarks of effective instruction is a teacher's ability to demonstrate to students how content is interrelated and how different subjects share characteristics and concepts while maintaining unique differences. Social studies is an umbrella for history, geography, economics, political science, communications, sociology, anthropology, art, and STEM. In reality, all subjects are umbrellas for smaller, more discrete areas that share commonalities. Yet, in academics, our cross boundaries, our interdisciplinary work is often degraded in favor of pure subject study. As teachers, we need to understand and clarify to students how different subjects inter-relate. We need critical thinkers and information-literate folks in the United States.

With the complexity and interconnectedness of the world, your role in teaching is the strategies and the processes of helping students understand how different academic fields are interrelated. Quality teaching is grounded in telling a complete and complex story simply. By creating exciting opportunities for students to understand how stem, social science, and the humanities play an interlocking almond complex role, you will provide tools and experiences beyond rote learning.

First, you start with your state's standards. Review these standards for whatever you are teaching. Then, look at the adjacent standards for your grade level. See what students are learning in other content areas. When you have read through those standards, you can see how adjacent areas interrelate and overlap. For instance, you may want to examine the concept of communicating about the author's purpose in ELA and social studies. Check how a letter or propaganda poster from world war I became part of the views people held long after the war about enemies of the United States. Then go and look at the debates about genetics from that time frame (1914-1918). Do you see the racism built into the "science" of genetics? Then look at the math: how many immigrants arrived in the United States, and what were their points of origin? Suppose you graph out the information and have students perform calculations, especially on forecasting. In that case, all this information created a horrible policy in the United States that cast immigration in a poor light and created blockages that led to devastating consequences for future discussions.

Second, you want to utilize team members and fellow faculty members. Never do the work alone. Always create a collaboration that will help students see how cross-curricular collaboration creates better, more authentic, and frankly engaging opportunities for students to learn and apply content-based skills in critical and in-depth manners. Teachers across and collaborating through curriculum conversation also add depth of knowledge to your areas of understanding and how you become a professional as pedagogical tips are shared. You may find yourself teaching maps (social studies and science) with comparisons to X and Y coordinates (in math). We have seen students struggle with statistics yet know how to calculate sports-based statistics.

This leads me to my third point: using your students' natural interests to guide lessons. Allowing students to work on interdisciplinary projects of their investigation and choosing is ideal. While it may seem difficult in the secondary levels, with proscriptive tests and state mandates, you may be able to allow students to create and implement a project that they find engaging within those standards and requirements. It would help if you also built upon your local resources, which I discuss in my book (Jakubowski, 2020), and help students use local knowledge and experiences to build community problem-focused efforts. One such area could be measuring the impact of beach or shore erosion after a storm. It would help if you had science, math, technology, and a little history, combined with reading and writing communication skills, to start your students by examining a local map of the water features within the community. Your local historical society or the National Geological Survey will have quadrangle maps that show land features. Then, you can have students create a historical presentation of what features they have noticed are altered over time. You can have students use their skills to graph the erosion rates and see if the rate has accelerated over time. They can compare this information with US Geological survey flood maps of the area and see if there are correlations. The students could then work with local environmental groups, town councils, or other public interest groups to share their findings with decision-makers or authors. You need to, as a teacher, find ways to engage your students across multiple content areas and teach skills founded on critical thinking and civic engagement. As information becomes more readily available, students need to focus on evaluation and implementation of argumentation instead of pure discovery and retention.

Activity Putting Tip #20 Into Action: Finding Ways to Engage Your Students Across Multiple Content Areas

Directions: Identify a thematic project you would like to work with your students to enact. Find your curriculum points across different standards that would meet that thematic area. Use the chart below to help you plan. Share your thoughts with your PLN with the hashtag **#50TeacherTipsBook**.

ELA	Math	Social Studies	Science

Art	Music	PE	STEAM

Ideas/content contained in the state standards of your state -or- professional association:

IRL (Reading/ Writing):

NCSS (Social Studies):

NextGen (Science):

NCTM (Math):

What are the themes my school asks me to cover in the grade level?

How can I collaborate with other teachers to teach themes across the curriculum?

How can I use a Know–Want to Know–Learned chart to gather student interest?

What resources are available to me? Casey recommends the C3 teachers (www.c3teachers.org) for social studies.

Tip 21: Bullying in the Building - What to Do If a "Colleague" Bullies You

The teaching profession is a people business. You are making a significant impact on the lives of others. You are part of a team and a professional, right? You will be mentored, valued, coached, and accepted as part of an ecosystem of collaboration in many places. However, some people did not, for one reason or another, get the email. You may have someone who isn't tuned in their way of speaking or working with others. Something the person says to you doesn't feel right, supportive, or collegial. The feedback is raw, unfiltered, or nasty.

A bully at school comes in so many different flavors. That person may make backhanded remarks about you to you or your colleagues. The bully may place passive-aggressive objects in your mailbox. The person may intentionally "forget" you about important events, announcements, activities, or opportunities. The behavior may include belittling you to students, colleagues, supervisors, parents, or community members. The bully may make sideways comments concerning everything from physical appearance, your professional practice or ideas.

In college, you learned a lot about how to work with students and give constructive and supportive feedback, but maybe not how to work with someone who isn't a team player. Remember, not everyone is or wants to be your friend, but people must treat you with dignity and respect. You are a human being and deserve basic dignity—end of story. If you feel that someone in your school is not exemplifying the basics of respect, dignity, and collegiality to you, seek out your mentor, and have a discussion.

Begin with a "naive question," asking a fundamental question. You may ask your mentor something like: "I'm wondering if I did something wrong? Mr. Jones seemed very dismissive of my lesson on numbers today."

If your mentor responds with something like: "Oh, that's just Mr. Jones. He's like that every day." You may want to ask a pointed question: "What do you think I should do? I didn't appreciate the way Mr. Jones was so dismissive."

Your second step is the hardest: ask the aggressor for a meeting, and request that the behavior stop. You may want to include your mentor if it helps you feel more comfortable. You want to begin by writing an email and explicitly requesting a meeting to discuss the behavior. Be sure to include the date, the time, and a description of the behavior.

At the meeting, use "I" statements such as: "I was uncomfortable with your tone and your words, and I feel concerned that our working relationship will suffer."

If the other person does not respond positively or their behavior escalates, walk away and immediately get to safety. You will want to document what has happened to your supervisor, the union, and human resources. You MUST be sure that you follow the District's human resources guidelines. Your mental, physical, emotional, and professional dignity and safety are paramount. Please remember, it's not you. It's them. You are probably not the only person who has had negative interactions or been bullied by the person.

Casey created a four-type bully system. The model may help you to understand the other person, but remember, YOU ARE NOT AT FAULT. In Casey's opinion, there are four types of bullies (Jakubowski, 2021), and these individuals can be categorized as unaware, unwise, out-lashing, and outcasts. He will briefly describe each type, with descriptions of behaviors. His feeling is that the first two do not understand how their actions impact others. The second two types know and are often in pain, needing professional help.

Four Types of Bullies

An unaware bully does not know that their behavior impacts others. The person does not truly understand what and how their interactions and behaviors impact others. This type of bully usually needs a confrontation and education to change their interactions with others.

An unwise bully may not understand social norms, and their behavior is unacceptable, as the person plays off the action, words, or event as a joke. The person knows that their behaviors are not acceptable but may believe that the activity falls within the "joke" or "dirty humor," or "risqué" humor models. These bullies, too, need confrontation and education to change their ways.

An out-lashing bully has often experienced pain in their own lives and, in a cry for help, is undertaking bullying behavior. When someone has an abused past and has learned abusive behaviors, the person is trying to regain control over their own lives by inflicting bullying on others. This type of bully may need professional help and systematic support to improve.

Outcast bullies are the most dangerous and challenging to deal with. This type of bully knows and still acts. This person intentionally tries to inflict pain on their victims with their behavior. This type of bully intentionally wants to be outside the society and may have a posse or gang to support them. While the person may have experienced their traumas in the past, they do not feel shame, discomfort, or desire to improve. This type of bully is hazardous and needs professional assistance.

Please know that you are not at fault. You are a victim, and you must take care of yourself. Seek out trusted friends and allies and, if necessary, the system that will ensure your workplace safety. You deserve it.

Activity Putting Tip #21 Into Action: Bullying Dialogue

Directions: Identify a situation you have seen or experienced. Create a dialogue to help you address what you did not like about that experience. Share your thoughts with your PLN with the hashtag **#50TeacherTipsBook**.

Tip 22: Planning for SEL

Should social-emotional learning (SEL) be included in lesson plans? Research suggests that it belongs in classrooms due to its variety of powerful benefits for students (Durlak et al., 2011; Jones, Greenberg, & Crowley, 2015; Taylor et al., 2017). However, there is little talk about SEL planning.

Teachers can agree that subject knowledge and content are essential in the classroom. Their lesson plans are focused on the content they will teach, the subject standard it addresses, and the pathway to demonstrate mastery of that content. There is no mention of a plan for integrating SEL into their lessons.

It is worthwhile to plan for SEL in the classroom. Prioritizing SEL is essential. If you plan for SEL, you make it a priority. It becomes a consistent part of your classroom when it becomes a priority.

How can SEL integration be effectively planned? At the time of this writing, it is uncommon, if not completely unheard of, to add SEL components to a lesson plan. Even though we expect it to become a trend in the coming years, now is the perfect time to change how you teach fundamentally.

This lesson plan template will guide you through the process of implementing an SEL plan. Plans can be implemented on a daily or weekly basis. Adapt it to fit your needs, but remember to develop a plan. Do not expect to walk into a class and hope a teachable moment arrives to bring up SEL topics. A well-thought-out plan can result in your students' most positive and sustainable outcomes.

Activity Putting Tip #22 Into Action: Planning for SEL

Directions: Complete this lesson plan template to plan for SEL in your lessons. Share your thoughts with your PLN with the hashtag **#50TeacherTipsBook**.

Element of SEL to target	*(from Casel.org)* -Self Awareness -Self-Management -Social Awareness -Relationship Skills -Responsible Decision-Making
Type of instruction	-Direct instruction -Whole class activity -Groups -1:1 conferences -Other
Programs/resources needed	-SEL Ed Tech -Worksheets -Books -Videos -Other

Time Allotted	
Further resources/extension activities	-Where can students further their learning on this topic?
Analyze & Reflect	-How will you analyze the impact of this lesson? -What can students do to reflect on what they learned? -How can you use feedback and data to inform you of the SEL needs and priorities of your students?

It will ensure that you are targeting specific aspects of SEL instruction with integrity and focus. Without a plan, it is easy to become overwhelmed by the day or sucked into content delivery. Although SEL increases students' ability to acquire knowledge, it is often overshadowed by the work needed to master skills.

When you're pressed for time or need to simplify, focus on the what and the how. What part of SEL will you teach, and how will you teach it? By holding a constant, immovable space for SEL instruction, you can further increase the outcomes for your learners.

Tip 23: Maximizing Your Planning Time

When Matt was a student teacher and in his first year of teaching, he always felt anxious about how much time it took to complete formal lesson plans. He had to write pages and pages of lesson plans. As they prepared him to understand the components of a lesson and instruction, he felt overwhelmed by having to plan lessons minute by minute with the mindset of striving for perfection for each lesson. During his first year of student teaching, Matt quickly learned that this was not practical, and he had to adjust my practice accordingly. He could still strive to have top-notch lessons but also had to take note of being efficient and manage his planning time. Ultimately, once Matt took a look at these practices regarding his planning and let them take hold, they revolutionized his teaching. We want this for you as well.

Planning is one of the most challenging aspects of teaching a class - at any grade level. It can be time-consuming, constantly changing, predicated on your students, and cooperative as it may require you to plan with your colleagues. Yet, it can also be one of the most interesting, fun, creative, and efficient things you do as an educator. Our goal is to provide a framework to help you navigate planning instruction for your students and several routines and habits that can help you become a practical and reflective planner.

Planning takes time. Teachers only have limited planning time regardless of whether they teach primary or secondary. Within a school day, there is only so much time teachers must utilize to dedicate to planning, outside other responsibilities that teachers have. Therefore, we must maximize our planning time because of the finite amount of time we have within a school day to plan.

To do this, we will provide tips to help you plan more efficiently. If you decide to implement several of these tips, we guarantee you will have more time and more organized and efficient plans for your daily and weekly lessons.

- Step 1: Organize Your Planning and Set the Intention - Organizing your planning is key to success. A planner or document will work, whether physical or digital. Additionally, find a location where you will always do your planning. Then, determine when you will plan daily. One great way to set the habit is to write down or say it consistently. An example would be, "After I get to school and sit down at my desk at 7:00 am, I will plan for at least 30 minutes before I work on anything else."

- Step 2: Long-Term Plan First Before Short-Term Planning - When planning, we first want to intentionally long-term plan before we short term plan. What does this look like? First, evaluate the standards you will want your students to reach after a sequence of lessons. Then, break down the standard into several objectives. Once this is done, develop the outline of the lesson sequence, starting with the assessments you will give. Following the development of the assessment outlines, you can begin scoping out the week's lessons by aligning each objective to the lessons. After you've set the objective, you can design the lesson for each day of the week. This lesson design includes how the lesson will be broken down, the instructional strategies used for the lesson, and the type of EdTech you may or may not use to help you facilitate the instruction.

- Step 3: Create Assignments, Tasks, Slideshows, and More - Once the design of the lesson and the long-term plan outline has been developed, you can begin creating the content for your lesson. This can include developing the template for the assignment, uploading it to your learning management system, and creating the slideshow or visuals you may want for your lesson. It can also include preparing manipulatives, math blocks, stations, or selecting the video your students may watch and respond to in teams. There are endless options within Step 3 because it's open-ended due to the standards and objectives you've selected and the long-term lesson outlines you have completed.

- Step 4: Place Content and Lessons into Folders - Once you have created the content for your lessons, you can place them into folders in your Google Drive or OneDrive account. To organize your lessons, use semester folders and then weeks. After this, you can have a digitalized long-term plan, as shown in Figure 23.1, with hyperlinks going directly to the content you've created for your lessons, which you can schedule on your learning management system, print, or display to your students.

Figure 23.1

Example Lesson Plan with Standards and Objectives for a Week of Math Lessons:

Standard(s) (Common Core State Standards Initiative, n.d.)

CCSS.MATH.CONTENT.5.NF.A.1

Add and subtract fractions with unlike denominators (including mixed numbers) by replacing given fractions with equivalent fractions in such a way as to produce an equivalent sum or difference of fractions with like denominators. *For example, 2/3 + 5/4 = 8/12 + 15/12 = 23/12. (In general, a/b + c/d = (ad + bc)/bd.).*

CCSS.MATH.CONTENT.5.NF.A.2

Solve word problems involving addition and subtraction of fractions referring to the same whole, including cases of unlike denominators, e.g., by using visual fraction models or equations to represent the problem. Use benchmark fractions and number sense of fractions to estimate mentally and assess the reasonableness of answers. *For example, recognize an incorrect result 2/5 + 1/2 = 3/7, by observing that 3/7 < 1/2.*

Objectives:

1. Students will be able to solve addition and subtraction fraction problems using the fraction buster technique at 75% accuracy.

2. Students will be able to solve addition and subtraction fraction word problems using the fraction buster technique at 75% accuracy.

Monday	Tuesday	Wednesday	Thursday	Friday
Math Lesson	**Math Lesson**	**Math Lesson**	**Math Lesson**	**Math Lesson**
Warm-Up Formative Assessment	**Warm-Up Formative Assessment**	**Warm-Up Formative Assessment**	**Warm-Up Formative Assessment**	**Warm-Up Formative Assessment**
Solving Addition Fractions	Solving Subtraction Fractions	Solving Addition Fraction Word Problems	Solving Subtraction Fraction Word Problems	Solving Fractions and Fraction Word Problems

Guided Practice	Guided Practice	Guided Practice	Guided Practice	Guided Practice
Modeling Addition Fraction Busters	Modeling Subtraction Fraction Busters	Modeling Fraction Busters in Word Problems	Modeling Fraction Busters for Subtraction Word Problems	Provide Feedback and Re-teaching
Independent Practice	**Independent Practice**	**Independent Practice**	**Independent Practice**	**Independent Practice**
Collaborative Problem Solving with Addition Fraction Busters	Collaborative Problem Solving with Addition Fraction Busters	Collaborative Problem Solving with Fraction Busters in Word Problems	Collaborative Problem Solving with Fraction Busters in World Problems	Practice and Reteaching Stations 1. Practice Problems 2. iReady 3. Small Group
Exit Slip Formative Assessment	**Exit Slip Formative Assessment**	**Exit Slip Formative Assessment**	**Exit Slip Formative Assessment**	**Exit Slip Formative Assessment**
Solving Addition Fractions	Solving Subtraction Fractions	Solving Addition Fraction Word Problems	Solving Subtraction Fraction Word Problems	Solving Fractions and Fraction Word Problems

- Step 5: Schedule and Print Content for the Lessons - One of the final steps is to schedule or print the content you've created. Scheduling content involves scheduling it on your learning management system like Google Classroom, Seesaw, or Canvas. This includes uploading the content and providing textual, visual, and auditory directions. Then, you will have the option to schedule its release to students during the scheduled day of the week the lesson will occur. Similarly, you can print all of your content and then organize it within physical folders for distribution throughout the week. One strategy to make printing as seamless as possible is to do it all at once throughout the week and organize the copies within Manila folders.
- Step 6: You're Ready to Teach - After following these steps throughout the week, you will be ready to teach. Remember, you can always go backward, forwards, or complete the steps before starting again. It may ultimately depend on your preferences or schedule. However, you will plan much more effectively and efficiently by taking each of these steps and intentionally doing them at a given time throughout the week.

Beyond these six steps, a few additional recommendations can further bolster your efficiency. Ultimately, we do not want you to reinvent the wheel every year if you do not have to.

- Reuse your content slightly to change it as you continue through the unit.
- Recycle content every school year by slightly refining it. Share and receive content from your colleagues and professional learning network.
- Do not reinvent the wheel. Use what works most often.

You can take steps to make planning more accessible and efficient. New and experienced teachers can all attest that planning takes much longer than anticipated. To maximize what we plan for our students, we must be intentional about when and how we plan. At the same time, we do not want to reinvent the wheel and over-plan. We were hoping you could develop a plan that works best for you and your students without going beyond the time allotted for planning. Use these steps and strategies in your physical and digital planner and develop routines to help you and your students cope with the stress of planning lessons.

Activity Putting Tip #23 Into Action: Plan Your Lessons For a Week

Directions: Using this template, plan a week of lessons using the strategies discussed in this tip to help you maximize your planning. Share your thoughts with your PLN with the hashtag **#50TeacherTipsBook**. Standard(s):

Standard(s):				
Objectives:				
Monday	Tuesday	Wednesday	Thursday	Friday
Lesson Topic Warm-Up Formative Assessment	Lesson Topic Warm-Up Formative Assessment	Lesson Topic Warm-Up Formative Assessment	Lesson Topic Warm-Up Formative Assessment	Lesson Topic Warm-Up Formative Assessment

Guided Practice	Guided Practice	Guided Practice	Guided Practice	Guided Practice
Independent Practice	Independent Practice	Independent Practice	Independent Practice	Independent Practice
Exit Slip Formative Assessment	Exit Slip Formative Assessment	Exit Slip Formative Assessment	Exit Slip Formative Assessment	Exit Slip Formative Assessment

Tip 24: Shining a Light on Self-Care

We must first pour into ourselves before we can pour into others as teachers. Let's talk about self-care. We all wish we had known more about this before starting our education careers. Self-care doesn't mean putting students on hold or delaying our work. By taking care of ourselves first, we can give to others and be the best teachers we can be.

Each person's definition of self-care depends on their preferences and stage of life. Sam, a full-time professor, wife, and mom, shares that self-care has been a journey for her as a teacher. Some things that she does to take of herself include:

- Blocking out all the other distractions or negative self-talk
- Scheduling time on her calendar to practice self-care
- Reading one book a month that is not related to education
- Exercise (at least 15 minutes a day)
- Taking a hot bubble bath every weeknight
- Getting out into nature and taking walks
- Spending time with family and loved ones (guilt-free)

Casey shares that as a faculty member, former classroom teacher, and school administrator, he struggled with self-care, and his emotional, physical health, and spirit suffered. He was always shooting for perfectionism when he should have been practical. He practices self-care by scheduling days intentionally away from the world of education. For instance:

- Join a social group AWAY from teachers, who explore local food places
- Try a sport like ax-throwing or bowling. Throwing stuff is fun.
- SLEEP: DO NOT UNDER ANY CIRCUMSTANCES sacrifice your sleep.
- Open and honest communication with your partner/ upfront discussions with a partner.

Very few professions have the level of stress that teachers deal with. A relationship partner must be willing to understand, adapt, overcome, and support you. Seek and utilize counseling services. You need to keep your mental health in good stead.

Kevin breaks self-care down into physical, mental, and emotional. Here are some strategies that he has found success in using:

- Physical
  - Heavy Lifting
  - Coaching (wrestling)
  - Going on walks
- Mental (discipline)
  - Early, consistent wake-up times
  - Occasional fasting (consult with a doctor first)
  - Challenges (training for a spartan race, 75 hard)
- Emotional
  - Daily Affirmations
  - Expressions of gratitude
  - Intentional time spent with loved ones

Matt practices self-care by:

- Going to the gym for a weekly class
- Riding his Peloton
- Going to the beach
- Cooking
- Enjoying new restaurants on occasion
- Traveling
- Spending time with friends and family
- Writing
- Podcasting
- Enjoying time with his puppies.

While each of these activities occurs throughout the month and year, Matt tries to take time out of the week and weekends to indulge in these activities, allowing him to focus on activities outside his day-to-day work. A regular rhythm of these activities creates a sustainable environment for Matt to do well in his various roles as an educator.

As teachers, it's imperative that we set boundaries and that we put time on our calendar for self-care. We all have things on our To-Do Lists or things we need to accomplish. We encourage you to put things on your list where you're taking the time to care for yourself. Plan half an hour or 15 minutes, whatever the time is during the day. Take care of yourself by doing something you enjoy that gives you joy.

There are so many ways to take care of yourself. Find out what works for you. We also encourage you to plan some self-care activities every morning, afternoon, and night so that we can hold each other accountable. What does self-care mean to you?

Activity Putting Tip #24 Into Action: Caring For You

Directions: Jot down ways you can take care of yourself during short and long periods. Also, schedule it into your day. Share your thoughts with your PLN with the hashtag **#50TeacherTipsBook**.

Day of the Week	Shorter Periods of Self-Care	Long Periods of Self-Care
Monday Morning Monday Afternoon Monday Evening		
Tuesday Morning Tuesday Afternoon Tuesday Evening		
Wednesday Morning Wednesday Afternoon Wednesday Evening		

Day of the Week	Shorter Periods of Self-Care	Long Periods of Self-Care
Thursday Morning Thursday Afternoon Thursday Evening		
Friday Morning Friday Afternoon Friday Evening		
Saturday Morning Saturday Afternoon Saturday Evening		
Sunday Morning Sunday Afternoon Sunday Evening		

Tip 25: Navigating and Managing Your Principal

Your principal will be one of the most influential figures in your school when you begin your teaching career. The principal is an educator, supervisor, and connection point in your educational organization. Depending on the size of your school, you may have an assistant principal and chairs at each grade level or department. You'll report to someone who will evaluate you, your work, and your tenure or contract renewal progress.

Within the school's ecology, the principal can be one of many different roles. In some principals, an amazing nurturing professional can guide the staff across significant events, leading to a team that evolves as a community of learning and caring. Often, the principal becomes the disciplinarian for the students and has little to do with curriculum and instruction. You may see the principal in their natural habitat: meetings. They are conducting meetings, setting agendas, facilitating discussions, and creating plans and programs for schools and the community. Principals have served as evaluators, often emerging from the office to walk the hallways and enter classrooms to see if teachers are implementing standards-based lessons. Quite often, a checklist or an electronic device exists under their arm, as observations are recorded, pictures taken, and impressions typed or scribbled.

As a novice teacher, YOU should remember this simple fact: the principal is a person too. You must follow one critical and crucial point: a human can be managed. You may wonder, *How? How can I, a new teacher, manage a seasoned professional charged with leading my school?* The reality is apparent: be prepared as a scout and have your work organized. The little points create the most significant concerns for principals. Remember, the name of your job is to do your best to keep everything from rising to the principal's attention.

First and foremost, always be prepared for your classes and be on time. Be ready to show well thought-out lesson plans tied to your school district's curriculum and your state's standards. Show how you planned those lessons by thinking through your reasons for teaching students those standards-based activities and capturing their learning in formative and summative ways. Demonstrate that you are engaging in data-informed instruction through the feedback of standards-based assessments and activities. Create lessons that are engaging for students, and if you are out of the classroom for some reason (professional or personal), these lessons should be implemented for a little learner disruption.

Second, address classroom management issues through proactive systems, rituals, routines, and a classroom culture that reinforces a community of learners and respect for all. You want to ensure that students know the entry and exit routines by week three. The students understand how the classroom operates, how to find information, and how to interact with you and your peers. By week five, the routine should be in place, and your students should be well motivated to work with you to engage in authentic learning.

Third, keep your work with parents on the heavy communication end. Now, you do not have to give out your cell phone because you will get texts and calls at all hours of the day. Instead, make sure to proactively send home email communications, update the parent portal, and proactively work with parents or home to ensure that communication is not just about issues but also is positive and reinforces what you want. You should make an effort to ensure that communication allows parents to understand if significant events, projects, or tests are happening and what the expectations for the students are. Realizing there are non-traditional families (split, blended, etc.) means the information could be lost, misplaced, or winds up in dad's car on mom's week; you may need to include two or more work sets for students.

Fourth, ask a naive question when you want to check with your administrator about a change or new idea. Try to broach the subject as a way to help the entire school. These conversations often start because you went to a conference, studied something in grad school, read about an idea in a professional magazine, or saw it on Pinterest, Twitter, Instagram, or whatever technology platforms are in use. A naïve question sounds like, "What do you think about XYZ?" or "I heard about ABC… what is your opinion?"

Fifth, no matter what, learn and grow. Take feedback, accept it gracefully, and try to improve your practice. Just remember that you will be asked to accomplish a lot. Take small steps towards becoming better. If you have a difficult situation, ask for help. If the principal is the situation, move on. You have many, many opportunities in education. Don't sacrifice your mental, physical, or emotional health for a job.

Activity Putting Tip #25 Into Action: Answering the Five Big Points Raised

Directions: Create a plan to implement the five points raised in the above section. Share your thoughts with your PLN with the hashtag **#50TeacherTipsBook**.

What is (are) my strengths?	Where Can I Improve?

How will I communicate the improvement?

Tip 26: Moderation is Everything: Celebrate the Highs, Mourn the Lows, and Moderate the Days

The excellent education world allows you, the teacher, to engage in a tremendous emotional rollercoaster. You will cheer for your highs, mourn your lows, and figure out a way to enjoy the year's marathon and, frankly, your career. As you work in the profession, you will expose your soul to a daily, weekly, monthly, and yearly engagement with people. People who need you to celebrate, mourn, and, most importantly, be the steady adult in their lives, no matter how much you want to exuberant or despair. Moderation, especially within emotion, is never easy. Casey shares, he still hasn't quite figured it out after 20 years. He still thrills at my students or my accomplishments. He resembles the *Parks and Recreation* character Chris Traeger, played by Rob Lowe, who always celebrated and mourned.

Just like the cliche of one practice, or game at a time, you must focus on one step in the process. Don't let the minutia get to you, but see the big picture and break it down into achievable steps. The year is genuinely ten months or more of grind, and you have to celebrate the good, mourn the bad, but moderate your in-between. There is a technique called setting SMART Goals, which may help you in your experience. First, establish specific, measurable, actionable, realistic, and timely goals. Think about how you will generate each part of the goals and how you will know you accomplish those goals beyond the emotion.

A SMART goal is a small part of a bigger picture. Within this goal, you will describe what you will do and why you will complete this goal. Maybe you would like to work with 20% of your class in moving to independent book selection in the school library. You will accomplish this feat by gathering data ahead of time. How do you know if you have met your SMART goal? You must have 20 percent of the class independently select a book in the school library. Our question is this: how many students could accomplish this task BEFORE you set the goal? If 100% of the class could independently select a book in the school library, you have a dud goal.

Several smart people have tough times setting SMART goals because they overthink it and don't practice or seek assistance in creating goals. Start by looking at SMART again: Specific, Measurable, Actionable, Realistic, and Timely. After you have gathered some base data about your class, you are now informed and can move to a gap analysis using tools and data gathering techniques. Using your state's standards and your district's curriculum, you can see where your students are in the present and the goal: where the students need to be by the end of school (usually 180 days later). You then establish a solid pathway for the class and build in what is referred to as formative assessments or checkpoints to see if your students are successfully progressing along the pathway. The checkpoints can also be signals for you and your class to celebrate. You can celebrate progress towards the goals. You can celebrate goal achievements. Don't self-criticize if you set a lofty goal that wasn't accomplished. Find the small wins, and most importantly, look at growth in the long run.

Journaling is a second way of measuring your wins, growth opportunities, and changes. Casey shares that he found writing a blog, which led to books, an intelligent way to express his feelings about the dissonance he experienced as a teacher (Jakubowski, 2020; Jakubowski, 2021). In journaling, you begin to reflect on what went right if you ask yourself the following questions:

- Which part of the lesson went well?
- When I established the bell ringer or hook, were my students engaged?
- Did my students understand the micro lesson I tried to teach?
- What questions emerged during the micro lesson that was not answered?
- Were the group activities explicit in direction and goals when I planned them?
- How supportive were each of the micro teams?
- When I closed the lesson, which parts were retained, and which were not?
- What did the data I gathered from the summative assessment demonstrate?
- How do my observations triangulate with homework, summative assessments, and others?
- What changes can I/ should I make?

You cannot do this level of in-depth analysis for every single lesson. You need to focus on one unit at a time and understand this: Japanese teachers who engage in this level of work receive 100% more release time for lesson study than American teachers (Seleznyob, et al., 2021).

Enjoy your time as a teacher. Remember to moderate the good, the bad, and what you would do differently. Keep positive affirmations flowing. This profession isn't easy, but you GOT THIS.

Activity Putting Tip #26 Into Action: Track Your Achievements

Directions: Create a chart of your achievements and areas for success. Name and date, and rate. On a scale of 1-100, what was the best? On a scale of -1 to -100, what was the worst? Do this for a few weeks (2-3). Share your thoughts with your PLN with the hashtag **#50TeacherTipsBook**.

Achievement	Date	Rate (Scale 1-100)

Tip 27: Having a Teacher Mindset of Success

You will hear the word "mindset" a lot. There is a great deal of research and practice surrounding practicing "mindset in education". There is a reason why it is stressed so often. The quality of your mindset impacts your job satisfaction, self-efficacy, effectiveness as a teacher, and even your joy and health. Having a success mindset is crucial.

However, mindset is more complex than catchphrases and inspirational quotes. Embodying a mindset of success takes regular practice, training, and dedication throughout the school year and summer. As with muscles, training will help you develop your mindset and create a positive trajectory. So how do you fit regular mindset training into your busy life as a teacher?

There are hundreds of successful methods of training your mindset. Therefore, it is not about "getting it right" but about growing and progressing. Remember, forward momentum in creating a mindset of success will benefit you and students and co-workers indirectly as they observe your positive example. Below are seven methods that can drastically improve your mindset as a teacher. This list is not exhaustive, and there are many positive strategies out there, but this will provide a strong starting point for you.

- Affirmations: Self-affirmations have been shown to positively impact self-efficacy and identity development (Cascio et al., 2016). Consistent practice in self-efficacy puts the teacher and person you want to be in the forefront of your mind, allowing you to progress towards that image. Find empowering phrases that build you up and say them daily before and after teaching.
- Gratitude: Gratitude is a fast track to happiness. The more you practice it, the easier it becomes to express and invite gratitude. In a job that is often thankless and full of stress, engage in the practice of gratitude daily. Find opportunities to show that you are grateful to the administrators, teachers, students, and parents you communicate with regularly.
- Optimism: Self-fulfilling prophecy is a concept discussed in many teacher prep programs. Optimism allows you to use it to your advantage. Believe in your students and your ability as a teacher. Look at challenging situations as opportunities to overcome. An optimistic outlook creates more success and helps you recover quickly from failures.
- Motivation Buttons: What motivates you? A daily, intentional dose of motivation can keep you inspired, even in the semester's most challenging and extended parts. Doodling, working on a passion project, or listening to inspirational videos - find the buttons you can press to motivate yourself. Then, make regular practice of it.
- Strong Habits: Habits are not often talked about in terms of mindset but are vital to it. A positive, enduring mindset is tough when you're eating and sleeping routine is thrown off, and your energy is low. Evaluate your habits. Drop the unhealthy or inconsistent habits that are holding you back. Give more life to the habits that keep you feeling fresh and energized.
- Purposeful Reflection: What did you do well? What can you improve on? Guide yourself in purposeful reflection at least once a week. It will teach you to be positive and accepting of your work while creating excitement for you to improve further. Reflection is not meant to beat yourself up, so keep your thoughts on praising what you have put in and progress for what you will do next.
- A Powerful Question To Ask: No matter how much you work on your mindset, teaching will provide you with tough and challenging days. On those worst days, try asking yourself the following question: "Why is this the best thing that could have happened?" That question forces you to go beyond the problem and consider the most positive and impactful results possible. It will fast-forward you to the solution and help you take as much action as possible to improve your situation.

The seven practices are achievable in a teaching day, but they can profoundly impact your career. The earlier you start prioritizing your mindset, the greater the benefits you will see.

Activity Putting Tip #27 Into Action: Mindset Matters

Directions: This reflection will help to maximize your mindset throughout the school year. Answer honestly and use it as a launching point for improvement. Share your thoughts with your PLN with the hashtag **#50TeacherTipsBook**.

What is your greatest strength in terms of your mindset? How can you make it even better?	
What is your biggest weakness in terms of your mindset? How can you reduce its impact?	
Who is the most mentally tough person you know? What do you admire about their mindset?	
What words or phrases can you use in front of your students to encourage a growth mindset in you and them?	

Critical Conversation Two: Critical Race Theory vs. Culturally Relevant Teaching

Critical Race Theory: The Boggart in the classroom.

Teachers and their choices in the classroom are under attack. First, state legislatures are passing laws about what can be taught in the classroom. Politicians are limiting the scope of curricular materials to eliminate anything related to a political "boggart" called Critical Race Theory (Milner, et al., 2021).

'So, the first question we must ask ourselves is, what is a Boggart?'

Hermione put up her hand.

'It's a shape-shifter,' she said.

'It can take the shape of whatever it thinks will frighten us most.' (Rowling, 2014, p. 92).

A boggart is an amorphous thing that scares people. Right now, some politicians are using CRT to scare people. Second, parents & interest groups are demanding that teachers educate children using traditional narratives which focus on white, middle-class values and experiences. Unfortunately, these attacks on academic freedom are not new and have a LONG standing tradition in America (Misco & Patterson, 2007; Scribner, 2016).

We need to distinguish between Critical Race Theory and Culturally Responsive Teaching, as both terms are considered by their opposition as unacceptable. Critical Race Theory emerged from legal and academic traditions as a process. It challenged how race and racial power are constructed and represented in American legal culture and, more generally, American society (Donnor, 2021, p. 262).

Critical race theory challenges the accepted and uninterrogated ways race and racial power is constructed in American society. The theory asks practitioners and academics to question why and how we view underrepresented people in places of power and how expectations, assumptions, and practices are unquestioningly assumed and transmitted.

Critical Race Theory is different from Culturally Responsive Teaching. It is defined as using ethnically diverse students' cultural characteristics, experiences, and perspectives as conduits for teaching them more effectively. It is based on the assumption that academic knowledge and skills are situated within students' lived experiences and frames of reference. They are more personally meaningful, have higher interest appeal, and are learned more efficiently and thoroughly (Gay, 2002, p. 106).

In other words, educators use their students' strengths and the local knowledge and experience the children bring to school to positively ensure students have a meaningful, successful, and informative learning experience. Examples include children's literature, which contains characters like the teacher's class members. I want to highlight the work of Moses (2021) as an example of a phenomenal children's book which describes the story of an African immigrant to America. Another example is using inclusive language within classrooms to describe communities. Teachers are challenged to remember that their culture and viewpoints are not the only ones. Their students do bring extraordinary lived experiences to the classroom. Research indicates that most American teachers are white, middle-class, suburban, and female (Redding & Nguyen, 2020). A positive note in the study did find more diversity in teachers, but still, the trend has not created a more balanced workforce.

One way novice educators can ensure their practice honors Culturally Responsive Teaching is through a wide range of resources for student use in the classroom and collaboration with their school or community librarian (Merga, 2020). Librarians are trained in the art of building resource collections that are appropriate for a wide range of students. The librarian professional is also a trained educator who can co-design units and provide opportunities for students to learn skills and abilities to seek materials for educational and recreational purposes.

Librarians are also trained in what to do if an educational resource is challenged (Rumberger, 2019). While a Board of Education can approve the selections of materials within their schools, book banning and censorship challenges bring national attention and often lead to community conflict. The interrelatedness of groups' desires to outlaw Critical Race Theory, ban books, and control what is taught in American schools is a concern (Goldberg, 2021). Fundamentally, the idea behind education is the creation of citizens who are information literate, critical thinkers, and collectively ready to create a society that embodies the ideas in American founding documents (as amended) of equal rights for all in opportunity.

So what should you do if a parent or a school official challenges your teaching decision or accuses you of teaching Critical Race Theory? First, take pride. Usually, when this happens, it means you are doing right by your students. Second, don't panic. You should ensure that your union representative (if you have one) is aware of the situation. If you teach in a state without union representation, you may wish to contact an advocacy group, such as the American Civil Liberty Union. You are probably not alone, and the entire school may be subject to public attacks or political maneuverings. If the entire school is under attack, watch closely what your school principal guides you. Contact the school safety coordinator or the local police if you are subjected to violent threats.

Consider this moment significant. Many educators who stood for what is suitable for their students had terrific, influential, and impactful careers. A particular blog post (Cisco, 2021) identifies five strategies teachers can use if accused of CRT. Communication and bridge building is critical in all five areas.

Remember, this isn't about education. It's about political power and influence… It's OK to be unsettled. It's not fair for educators to be wrapped up in something like this, mainly when we're surviving a pandemic and distance/hybrid learning (Cisco, 2021).

Our dialogue dives into the classroom application of culturally responsive education:

Matt: I would say creating a culturally responsive classroom is establishing and maintaining a welcoming and affirming environment. It's my opportunity to build close relationships with students and families by being an active listener and spending time with them over time, and learning about their lived experiences, along with being someone in their lives who can teach them some skills and some content. Additionally, it's about being inclusive and providing opportunities for all types of learners by meeting them where they're at, differentiation, and support to all students, whether they are of a different culture, race, or background or have a different ability to learn they're generating gender identification. It's providing an inclusive environment for students and, additionally, it is providing an opportunity for them to learn skills and content with me having high expectations of them to grow as human beings, not just as learners place humans and provide that opportunities for example in my class, you can do project-based learning where students work together as teams on a specific issue or topic and that allows us for students have different types of leadership opportunities different levels of student classroom engagement. It can be differentiated from my listeners, so that's just an example of culturally responsive teaching in my classroom.

Kevin: I think the thing that I lean on is where Paulo Freire (1970) talks about education and says, you know you're reading the word and the world. And that's what I try to remember when I position myself in a classroom: I'm somewhere between teaching students about the society they live in and learning about the community and the culture they live in. At an individual, family, and local community level up - we must understand that all of those perspectives are valid and vital to the classroom and the learning of the entire classroom. Understand that I try to place myself as much as possible in a co-learning situation where I'm not projecting information down to my students, and I'm not dissertating my ideas straight to their faces. Instead, we're working together and learning, where I might connect them to specific content knowledge. Still, I also want to connect to their lived experiences and understand where those moments intersect. How can I help bridge that gap and learn with you to experience this in a new way, so you know I might speak with every English teacher class about similes and metaphors? But, that might mean something very different in terms of how we connect with that content, and you know what projects, what disciplines, what methods we use to get that knowledge together rather than me just dictating the knowledge.

Sam: A classroom is where a child should feel safe, valued, and appreciated. With a culturally responsive classroom, we can do just that. It's a space that challenges and supports students where they are in their learning. A classroom is where learning happens, and differences are accepted, not pushed aside. We all learn and grow differently. That is a beautiful thing.

Kevin: How do we reframe the conversation for culturally responsive teaching?

Casey: I was angry when I went to college, and I had heard all through my elementary, middle, and high school about the "ever upward" American history narrative. Yet, in college, data, information, and other debate points were raised, and I thought: Why was I not exposed to this earlier? Culturally responsive education does teach children that our nation isn't perfect. So, how should educators balance the need to educate our students while making them simultaneously? Comfortable in the discomfort of the reality that change takes time and America isn't perfect?

Kevin: So, I think about a moment I had in a class and one of my first years of teaching, and on September 11, 2001, you know, much further past the tragedy, and we had an open and honest dialogue about not only what happened, but what it meant. For people in our country (the United States), in terms of fear, safety, and perceptions. One of my students commented, "I thought all Muslims were terrorists." Knowing this class very well and the students very well, I understood at that moment he was saying it very genuinely. He didn't believe that what he was saying was shocking or newsworthy because that was his context, and that's what he knew.

One other student in the class turned to the other student and said, "You know I'm Muslim," and the first student replied, "well, I didn't realize you were a terrorist." At that moment, as the teacher, I realized, "I don't think the first student is conceptualizing what words like 'Muslim terrorists' actually mean." We, as educators, have an obligation as educators to address these uninformed utterances. Still, these exchanges don't often get addressed in a classroom and in a moment in a middle school where students are hearing utterances and need context, depth, and perspective. Students might say things that to an individual are meaningless but carry much more critical weight to the person receiving those words, creating fear and a lack of safety for the student who hears these utterances go unchallenged or addressed. So, I think that's the result of not having conversations about race, not having conversations about culture, and not bringing up these topics in classrooms. A hazardous environment occurs when topics of diversity are absent from the classroom. Some parents who complain about teachers tackling topics concerning diversity, culture, and difference, make the classroom a depressing or dangerous, or scary place for their students.

The parents who object do not realize that not bringing these crucial topics up makes it even more fear-inducing for other students and creates a moment where the purpose of public education is lost. Avoiding these conversations with students creates dangerous repercussions that grow as they age. We must discuss complex subjects to create a safer and more inclusive environment for all students and better education opportunities.

Casey: Kevin, I think you said something so profound, and I want to stop for a second and make sure that people read this correctly: your child is not more important than every other child. We have become a society where we do not recognize that we must teach every child.

Matt: I believe that words in actions matter in a classroom. For our students to understand the issues we face, they are far more complex than a black and white argument. Providing them with these ideas of having a conversation with someone when the issue is not black and white is important by giving them those skills and providing them that confidence and safe space to ask someone these questions openly and for students to have the skills as well as building not only their academics but their emotional intelligence to handle conversation by talking about race, talking about gender identity, gun policy and gun safety, and political issues.

Having that confidence, emotional intelligence, and most importantly academic skills, we must have these civic conversations in the classroom. This is the beginning of where these can take place and also builds empathy for others because the words that we say mean different things to other people and have those conversations with other people. That may be different from us. They must tell us about their lived experience, which is one of the strategies I like to do. Throughout my classrooms, whether it's teaching English, teaching social studies, or even teaching that Socratic seminar. Openness and building that culture within your classroom to begin these conversations and it can start early on because this strategy can be something that can be done from late elementary up through graduate school. Hence, it's something to be aware of and build that culture in your classroom where students understand that words matter, actions matter, and issues are not two-sided or cut and dry. They're very complex and can be broken down and then openly discussed.

Final Thoughts - Critical Conversation #2

At the root of our roles as educators, we must ensure that all students are welcome in our classrooms. As our demographics change, we must teach children to assume a civic role in the diversity of the United States. While Critical Race Theory is a political flashpoint in the 2020s United States, classrooms are engaged in Culturally Responsive Teaching. We value and honor the traditions and heritage of all our students. We ensure classrooms are open, welcoming, and safe discussion places. We work with all students of all nations, and we create a community of learners who see the strengths in everyone.

We, as educators, must address the scourge of hatred and end the evils of deliberate denigration. We create value spaces through shared learning, everyday experiences, and a culture of care for everyone. We go beyond the surface and embrace the depth and complexity of our changing America. We celebrate the achievements, study the failures, and plan to improve our nation as a citizenry. We educate our children, inform our adults, and collaborate to inspire our communities to embrace all peoples. We are not afraid. We embrace change and complexity in our community.

SECTION 3: THE TOUGH GET GOING

January   February

March

"You don't have to have it all figured out to move forward... Just take the next step." - Anonymous

Section 3: The Tough Get Going

A joy from childhood: FIRST SNOW DAY. Unless you have online schooling that day (boo.) You have just finished the holiday break this time of the year, and the New Year is emerging for the LONGEST STRETCH OF NON HOLIDAYS. Yikes! We bring you the "grind' of the year. Some may switch as semester courses end, and new ones begin if you are a secondary teacher. For most teachers, you may see an upswell of student transfers as contracts expire in the business world. Do not forget to re-engage with classroom culture- any break longer than three days, and students forget. You will also start seeing worrisome patterns as students struggle, and you may need to begin recommendations for remediation or retention. You also need to ensure you are practicing self-care-the nights were short, but now the bitter cold kicks in, and yucky, those raging storms will make commuting difficult. Also, think about how the graduate school semester ended and how a new one started. You also made it to Round 2 of parent-teacher conferences. Try to anticipate what vacation you will treat yourself to during spring break. For new teachers, staycations are fantastic. Maybe see some relatives. Try going to a tea or coffee club. You may enjoy the company.

Tips and Strategy Entries 28-40

Tip 28: Developing Equity for Sanity's Sake

Equity work has been among the most consuming topics in schools, pre-service prep programs, and politics for the last several decades. What is equity? As a teacher you need to ensure all of your students have opportunities, and engagement with a curriculum and practices designed to enhance, not restrict their future! Equity pedagogy links to increased student success, higher test scores, student well-being, and more (Walden & Baxley, 2017). Amidst all of the benefits, it remains controversial as politicians and leaders debate the appropriateness of equity work in a classroom setting. This tip will not go into the debate but rather give a different and unique reason to embrace and apply equity pedagogy in your classroom. Equity work improves the sanity of the teacher.

A teacher's day is packed with decisions and responsibilities. Teachers have an overwhelming number of conversations and interactions throughout the day. As a result, many focus on the academic side of teaching. Focusing simply on content and nothing else eliminates various distractions that pull at their energy. A neutral view of students and their relation to the curriculum may make the teacher's job easier to manage and less stressful to enact.

However, breaking this topic down reveals that it does the opposite. By narrowing the teaching day to a strictly academic focus, teachers create an environment where students cannot maximize their success. The teacher cannot understand the barriers to the success of their students and where the joy of relationships and co-learning cannot flourish. This environment is an unstable work world filled with stressors. This factor is why we posit equity pedagogy contributes to the sanity and well-being of teachers who engage in the practice.

Having taught over 1,000 students, Kevin shares that he has yet to hear any of them say that they want to do poorly in school, be in trouble, or get bad grades. Yet, many students find themselves unexplainably in that situation. There is a disconnect between the student some hope to be and the performance and outcomes they receive regularly. This disconnect cannot be examined in a classroom that remains neutral, includes no room for equity, and focuses solely on academic achievement. Students begin to feel lost, not understanding where their disconnect comes from in an environment that does not allow them even to question it.

Likewise, teachers may become incredibly frustrated by the unrealized potential of their students. Seeing students capable of greatness within academics be held back by an invisible force is painful. That is what it feels like when equity is removed from the room. Removing student narratives and drowning out student voices creates a network of blind spots for teachers. Authentic equity pedagogy in a classroom eliminates those blind spots. It creates a complete picture and scope of each student, the barriers that interrupt their success, and actionable steps to create an environment that nurtures rather than hinders their growth.

Lastly, a lack of focus on equity pedagogy means a lack of genuine relationships with your students. By removing the identities and characteristics of the students in your classroom, you may only ever know a shell of who they are. You may learn of their hobbies but have no idea why it is a passion for them or their family. You may hear of an unfair moment that upset them but miss the racial/social/gender / etc. injustice that created that and future moments. Meaningful student relationships go beyond simply "being kind" or lending an ear. A strongly fostered relationship with students must allow room for their lived experience and an analysis of their narrative alongside the world surrounding them.

Your well-being as a teacher relies on the removal of frustrations and misunderstandings. If each day is spent pounding content into a room full of people you do not have a deep understanding of, do not care about, and are not invested in you, your success and happiness will dwindle. Conversely, a classroom engaged in equity pedagogy has the bravery and courage to grow as co-learners in a shared space. A teacher who removes the natural barriers that a strictly academic class puts up will have more fulfilling, dynamic, and engaging daily dialogue. They will receive the educational benefits of exploring and analyzing the impact of equity among their students. Still, they will also receive the personal benefits of a work environment filled with love and empathy.

Activity Putting Tip #28 Into Action: Track Your Achievements

Directions: Consider your role as a co-learner. Pick an upcoming lesson you have planned (or are about to plan). Add the following sections to your lesson plan and respond to them. Share your thoughts with your PLN with the hashtag **#50TeacherTipsBook**.

- What unique strengths do my students have that will help them contribute to this lesson?

- What opportunities will I give students to connect this lesson to their lived experiences?

- Who are my resources in the community that can explain the concept, stress its importance, or show the concept in action? How can I give my class access to that person/people?

- What is my unique perspective on this topic, and how may I encourage my students to share and voice their perspectives?

Tip 29: Finding Mentors To Support and Empower Your Teaching Career

Matt shares, "My journey in education began with little to no mentors. I had mentors in other facets of my life, including my late grandfather, high school basketball coach, and political science professor from undergrad. I had no contacts or mentors in education when I decided to become a teacher. Looking back, it felt daunting as I did not have anyone in education to discuss it with and help guide me. Yet, mentors did arise as I continued through my teacher preparation program. However, I did not have a solid mentor when I went into my first year of teaching. I had support. But not a mentor."

He shares this outline of his early career for several reasons. First, it's because mentors are fluid in your life. What does that mean? Having mentors and undergoing mentorship is constantly changing in your life and career. At one time in your life, mentors may come and go. Sometimes, mentors stay relevant and a part of your life for a long time. However, they may not be as relevant in your career or life experience. Although, one crucial facet about all of this stands out: it's about relationships. Additionally, it ultimately depends on the circumstance and time in your life when they appear. Yet, it's about your ability to cultivate relationships at the right time.

When Matt went through his teacher education, he had three professors whom he looked towards for mentorship. One of them continues to be a mentor and colleague from time to time. He didn't bond with his guide teachers as he began student teaching. As a teacher, he had colleagues whom he asked for support but were not mentors throughout my early career. Later, as he connected with more educators and continued his education, mentors appeared again. Then, years later, he connected with several educators through my professional learning network, resulting in several mentors he continually reached out to and worked on projects.

Much of the research on mentorship and educators provides insight into the power of mentors. Educators who have mentors generally tend to stay in the profession longer than those who do not. The critical element is that the mentee feels supported and empowered by their mentor and the environment they are teaching and leading in. This concept is not only for new teachers. It's for all teachers who have years of experience and novices.

I talk about my experience with mentors before jumping into ideas of how to find a mentor because the reality is that mentors will come and go in your career. Going through your career is daunting without one or a group of trusted colleagues you respect and truly value their advice and support. Although, by building relationships and expanding your local and global professional learning network, you will find yourself having many mentors at the right time for many facets of your career. Ultimately, mentorship provides opportunities for community and guidance. Someone who can be your cheerleader, guide and encourage you to grow in your career, and help you navigate challenging situations and problems you may encounter. The goal is to describe several strategies to help you find mentors and build relationships with them so they can uplift you and you can uplift others through your mentorship.

How to Find Mentors

Let's first discuss how you find mentors and build relationships with them. Then, we will outline ways to find mentors who may not live or work in your setting. Both are important because they offer different forms of mentorship that can impact you in multiple ways.

Finding local mentors involves building relationships with colleagues and other educators within your local sphere. They may be teachers within your school, district, or neighboring district. Mentors may be a professor you've built a strong relationship with. Or a mentor could be with an administrator with which you have grown close. It could even be someone who works at the central office. Ultimately, there can be a wide variety of educators to choose from.

Now, let's focus on finding a mentor, followed by actions you can do to cultivate that relationship and experience with them. Here are some steps to think about as you think about finding a mentor and building your relationships with others in the profession.

Have a Clear Idea of Your Goals in Finding a Mentor

What goals do you have in finding someone who can support and cheer you on? Do you want to build your capacity? Do you want to support yourself in navigating your first few years of teaching? Do you want someone to help you reignite that spark? Do you want someone to talk with during good and challenging times? All of these variables are important to take into consideration. Yet, the goal is to have a clear vision of how someone can help you and use their life experiences to mentor you in yours.

Finding the Right People - Building Relationships

First, recall that you can have more than one mentor. Connecting and building relationships with many other people is incredibly important. Building professional relationships begins with listening and asking questions. Be present. Focus on what they are saying and ask follow-up questions that may provoke an insightful response. You can ask them personal questions related to the experiences you may be going through at this moment. Over time, you can evaluate whether the person is someone you would like to get to know better. Understand whether the person can help you develop your strengths and areas of improvement professionally and personally.

Additionally, determine whether they may be a person who wants to cultivate a relationship with you by giving their own time to spend with you. Once these questions have been answered, you can put forth the time and commit to getting to know this person better and begin to trust them and their insight. After you feel comfortable with them, you can ask them to be your mentor. Or, it can happen organically through your conversation with them over time.

Show Them You Value Their Feedback

Working with a mentor requires the mentee to take action and demonstrate that the mentor's feedback is helping guide them. After meeting with the mentor, demonstrate their advice with action that you can show them to receive more feedback. Additionally, in the same light, provide your mentor with feedback regarding their advice and illustrate how you value their feedback. For example, your mentor discusses how you can get involved in the School Site Council to learn more about school culture and see how you may be able to use those funds for your classroom. Your goal would be to attend a meeting or two and report back. While reporting back, you can outline what you've learned and your appreciation for their feedback. You can be honest as well. If you feel it may not be as helpful, you can discuss it with them. However, please demonstrate that you value their guidance and feedback as the follow-up conversation regarding this event may lead to even greater insight.

Make it Easy for Your Mentors - Show Gratitude

One way to ensure you cultivate your relationship with your mentor is to show them gratitude for their time. This can include a verbal phrase, giving them a gift, or helping them with a project. Our words and actions are essential, and showing Gratitude helps reinforce and build the mentee and mentor relationship you both have

Finding Mentors Outside Your Local Area - A Professional Learning Network is Key

We will now focus on finding mentors outside your local school and district. We have a global community of educators who share many of your values and goals in education. What's fantastic about having a global professional learning network (PLN) is that you can connect and grow with educators worldwide. By growing your PLN, you may have an opportunity to find a mentor and utilize them as a helpful resource to further your career.

To find a mentor with a PLN means we must first build our PLN. Growing your PLN heightens the chance you may find someone you want to connect with who can eventually become a mentor. All of the same principles outlined above still apply. However, groundwork must occur before finding a mentor in the greater educational community. Here are several steps you can engage in to do so.

- Engage in Twitter Chats and join educator groups on Facebook - Grow Your Network.
- Follow Educators Who Share and Do Not Share Your Same Values and Experiences
- Review Their Posts and Content & Respond to Them
- Determine If You'd Like to Connect
- Send them a Direct Message
- Build the Professional Mentor and Mentee Relationship

Over time, with the growth of your PLN, you may build relationships with educators who may become mentors to you. Ultimately, you may have many mentors that are a part of your PLN. Therefore, it's essential to cultivate your PLN and critical relationships within it as it may reap benefits to help amplify your growth as an educator.

Having mentors can be game-changing for your career. However, recall that having mentors in your life and career is fluid, meaning as you grow and transition as you progress through your career, mentors may come and go.

Thus, it's important to find many mentors in your career. You rarely have a mentor that will stay in your realm your entire career and remain relevant. By finding mentors that can help cultivate you and grow your capacity as an educator and person through observations, coaching, and connecting with your mentor's professional learning network, you will have more opportunities to grow and learn. Additionally, you can harness the networks you create through your local and global mentors. Ultimately, you may have several mentors and maybe mentors for other educators in your local and global networks, which amplifies your impact and work.

Activity Putting Tip #29 Into Action: Finding a Mentor

Directions: Write down a list of possible mentors you believe could fit that role. Then, write down WHY you think they may be a good mentor for you. Last, determine how you are going to contact and connect with them. Share your thoughts with your PLN with the hashtag **#50TeacherTipsBook**.

Possible Mentors	Why Would They Be a Good Mentor?	How Will I Connect With Them?

Tip 30: Protecting Our Digital Presence as New Teachers

Your digital presence as an educator is a virtual handshake that employers, families, and students can see 24/7. Your digital presence doesn't include only what you post but also what you share, repost, like, and comment on. So be choosy and think before you post online. It would be best if you protect your digital presence positively and professionally. Be protective of what you put out there online. We encourage you to tell your own story. If this idea is new to you, we recommend starting as a learner on a social media platform (Fecich, 2018).

For example, create a Pinterest account or Instagram account. Look to see what others are posting and save ideas for later. Or comment on what someone else shared. Next, share an idea you have or have tried in the classroom. You can also harness your digital presence by creating a digital portfolio. A digital portfolio is a great space to showcase all you've been doing in and out of the classroom. You may be required to create a digital portfolio as a part of your first year as a teacher. Additional ways to harness your digital presence:

- Do a Google search for yourself
- You should be selective about who you follow online. You should follow people who will provide you with new ideas, encouragement, information, and resources you can use, as well as positive messages.
- Create a professional Instagram or Twitter profile
- Social media is a great way to share what you are doing in the classroom
- Use Pinterest, Twitter, and Instagram to find classroom ideas
- Take part in a Twitter chat
- Watch a live Instagram video about an educational topic
- Connect with others on LinkedIn by creating an account
- Follow trending educational hashtags and use them in your posts.

Activity Putting Tip #30 Into Action: Creating an Educator Social Media Account(s)

Directions: Getting on social media is easy. Pick a space where you want to share and learn more about education. Start by first learning about the platform and from others using it. Then, make a plan to start to share what you are doing and learn about 3x a week. Drop ideas below with what you can share about on social media. Share your thoughts with your PLN with the hashtag **#50TeacherTipsBook**.

1.	2.	3.
4.	5.	6.

Tip 31: What Do We Do With Phones?

Phones have changed the landscape of education. As technology gets smaller and more portable, students have access to the internet, communication, gaming, and more. This concept leads to many issues that include classroom distractions, a loss of focus, cyber-bullying, illegal activities, the recording and posting of the teacher, and anything that happens within the classroom space. With all the issues spiraling around the phone, teachers must have a plan to deal with classroom phone use.

Once hired, you may find that your school has a consistent policy for student phone use. Some facilities ban phones outright, while others allow free use and do not allow teachers to confiscate phones from students. These policies vary greatly and can impact your approach to phone use. However, having a plan for handling technology in your classroom is still crucial.

Phone policies in the classroom are one part philosophical and one part practical. You may feel as though you would like to take away every phone that causes a distraction but find that it takes your time and energy to apply it. Or you might try allowing phone use and teaching responsibility, only to find your class trending on TikTok with much-unneeded attention to your teaching. It would help if you considered alignment with many different values on phones in the classroom. Whatever your values are, they must match their practical application in your classroom. If it is unmanageable, it will not stick.

If your students have phones and your school does not have an outright ban on them, you will indeed find them in your classroom. It may be surprising how many phones you will see, even at young grade levels. Instead of thinking of all the ways to eliminate the phone issue, it may be more beneficial to consider how you can leverage phones in your classroom. Here are three ways Kevin allowed phones in his classes to enhance the student experience, rather than fighting to eliminate them.

Reward Leverage

Teachers can leverage phones for a reward in straightforward ways. It could be as easy as, "finish your work, and you can play on your phone for five minutes between tasks." This idea is a weaker form of motivation, but you can implement it quickly to provide a boost to your class. Unregulated phone time can be offered upon completing a task if you lack energy and enthusiasm. It also allows you to set healthy boundaries about keeping phones to yourself, using headphones or no volume, and being respectful of the work area and space of others.

Work Leverage

While phones are often looked at as devices made for fun, incredible productivity tools are available to students. Instead of wearing yourself out trying to get rid of phone usage, it may be time to incorporate phones into your coursework. Students can produce deep research on the class content, find relevant videos, and even make and record video responses to content. The technology that is available for class use is innumerable and widely influential. (An important note: A reliance on phones for classwork should be accompanied either by the availability of technology like laptops on-site or with group work to ensure that students who do not have phones will be able to participate)

Feedback Leverage

A significant and often underestimated reason for allowing phones in the classroom is to gain valuable feedback. Students often remark that their voice goes unheard in class settings. Technology can create an easy outlet to see, monitor, and act upon. Some programs allow communication in various methods, whether to safely text the teacher without sharing numbers, to check in on students' mental health and well-being, or even to gain quick, insightful feedback on lessons, pacing, and class structure.

You may want to take a strict stance on phone use. However, it is a fantastic idea to be prepared to leverage phones for the betterment of your classroom. If they are in your room, find a positive function for them. Otherwise, phones will become a source of frustration and interrupt your curriculum.

Activity Putting Tip #31 Into Action: Designing Your phone policy

Directions: Create and use the following lists to help design your classroom technology policy. Share your thoughts with your PLN with the hashtag **#50TeacherTipsBook**.

Create a list of apps/programs that add value to your class.	Create a list of fears and worries you have about tech use.	Use those two lists to create an acceptable use policy that encourages the positive use of phones while minimizing the distractions they may cause.

Tip 32: Formative Assessment is Easier Than Ever Before in History

With the help of EdTech tools such as Pear Deck, Nearpod, Buncee, and Whiteboard.fi, Google Forms, Kahoot, Quizizz, Quizalize, and Formative (among many others), we can see student progress. We can even see students solving problems and completing tasks in real-time with some of these tools. As a result, not only after the formative assessment has been completed can we provide feedback in real-time for our students. Therefore, we can analyze the whole class and individual student progress more accessible than ever to improve our instruction and feedback.

Formative Assessment Equals Formative Feedback

As mentioned above, formative assessment in today's world equates to formative feedback. Sometimes this feedback can be done in real-time or strategically throughout a lesson on a personalized whole-class basis. For example, after students complete a warm-up activity or problem using Pear Deck, we can narrow in on things a student did well on and errors and mistakes students may have made. These feedback points can be discussed directly with the class immediately after completing the problem. Teachers can also provide feedback throughout the assessment process if several students are stuck. Feedback can be utilized as a scaffold in this example to help spark further problem-solving. With the help of EdTech tools like Pear Deck, we can provide this valuable feedback within any classroom setting, which can amplify student learning.

Formative Assessment Strategies Infused with Tech - Interactive Slides

There are some times within a lesson you can incorporate a formative assessment. Now, more so than ever, teachers can deploy formative assessment techniques at any time during a lesson, and results can be provided immediately, allowing us to modify our instruction. Several strategies can help us do that and gather information on our students to cultivate relationships with them further. Let's dive into each of these strategies and quickly summarize them.

- Think, Write/Solve, Pair, and Share - Students can be assessed in many ways. First, on their initial response and solve the problem, and after they collaborate with a partner. Then they share it with the rest of the class.
- Warm-Up or Exit Slip - At the beginning or end of class, students complete a set of problems or are asked to complete a prompt for writing. Students submit the answer, and the results are given to the teacher. In real-time, feedback is given to the entire class based on how students did on the assessment.
- Adaptive Assessment - Students are given an adaptive assessment that meets them where they are in terms of what they know. For example, using a tool like iReady, students can be assessed on a wide range of topics where they are assessed where they are at based on their history of completing previous assessments on similar topics. Students can be assessed on the same topic, but their assessment is adapted to meet their learning needs.
- Game-Based Assessment - Students within a class can be given a formative assessment that is not graded, whereby they compete with each other. Using EdTech tools like Kahoot and Quizizz, students can compete against one another as they review and are assessed.
- ClassTools.net is an EdTech treasure trove from a QR code generator and random name picker to Fakebooks and fake Twitter. The tools on classtools.net can encourage students to thrive and perform well in a classroom environment.
- With Canva, students can create custom posters to show what they know. The students will be able to see their work displayed in the classroom.
- Flip - Flip can be used across the curriculum and grades to record videos. The first step is to create a class grid. Grids serve as a hub or meeting place for video discussion. They store topics for discussion. Once a topic is selected, you can customize it with many options. Then share the link with students. Students are free to record their responses on any platform. Imagine all the possibilities if you could record a response.

- Sway is a tool that allows you to create animated flyers embedded on a class website or linked to in an email. A Sway can include images, text, links, videos, embed codes, and audio. You can also customize color schemes and designs. Teachers can use sway in various subject areas to create digital newsletters, letters to parents, or reports and presentations.
- BookCreator The popular iPad app is now available on Chrome and Canva EDU. The next step is to select the book's layout. You can upload images from your computer or the internet. The book can also include text, shapes, drawings, and voice recordings. E-books can be published online or downloaded by students. Students can create books about themselves to introduce themselves to the class, or they can create book reports they can share online. You can have students write about a historical figure or a country. The possibilities are endless with Book Creators.

We live in the age of formative assessment. We can deploy assessments quickly and effectively and provide feedback to our students, and monitor and adjust our instruction to meet our students where they are at. Now, more than ever, we can do this in any classroom setting. It has been game-changing and has revolutionized how we give an assessment, amplifying how we can give our students feedback. Navigating and implementing formative assessment is essential to amplify our instruction and student learning within our classrooms.

Activity Putting Tip #32 Into Action: EdTech Exploration

Directions: These are just a few EdTech tools to use with your students for formative assessment. Use the space below to research a few tools and try them out in your classroom. Share your thoughts with your PLN with the hashtag **#50TeacherTipsBook**.

EdTech Tool	Strategy for Classroom Use for Formative Assessment

Tip 33: Keeping Up with Professional Learning - Professional Development For You By Teachers

A PLN or a professional learning network is one of the tools a new educator should have in their toolbox. See Tip #3 for more information. PLNs challenges teachers to really become engaged in education and learning. First, a PLN stands for a personal (or professional) learning network. You turn to your PLN when you have questions about teaching or wish to share ideas; it doesn't just happen online. You can also meet in person.

Additionally, you can connect with people across the country and even worldwide. Fecich (2018, 2019) shares, create a professional account on the platform of your choice. You get access to tons of excellent resources that you can use now that you are in school preparing. You can learn what interests you at your own pace. Teachers use it to guide their professional development. Connecting with other educators can give you a sense of belonging and community that can help you get through those stressful days. Your PLN can be a great source of support for future educators. Some must-haves for your professional bio:

- Professional photo
- A professional username is required.
- A professional email to direct all formal inquiries.
- Use hashtags in your bio to show who you are as a teacher.
- You can use copyright-free images in your header.
- Consider hashtags that speak to your teaching heart.
- Review hashtags that relate to content that you want to learn more
- Please look at who's posting, read their bio, follow them, then see who they're following.
- Retweet or share a post by someone else
- Comment on a post by a colleague
- Participate in a Twitter chat. They take place almost every day of the week. It's like a conversation that covers all kinds of education-related topics. Choose a chat that interests you. Second, ensure the chat is happening by reaching out to the moderators. Third, engage in conversation and connect with other participants. We recommend using Tweetdeck to keep organized with posts, replies, and more when participating in a Twitter chat.

As an educator, you have so many opportunities to connect with others around the country and worldwide to help you grow.

Activity Putting Tip #33 Into Action: Hashtag Searching

Directions: Take some time to scroll through Twitter or Instagram. Jot down a few hashtags that pique your interest. Share your thoughts with your PLN with the hashtag **#50TeacherTipsBook**.

Tip 34: Separate Your Personal and Professional Life

In education, allowing the all-consuming nature of the profession to overwhelm your identity is super easy. Your first challenge will be this: maintaining boundaries. Why? It is so good for your mental, physical, and social health. The reality is teaching is never done, during the year and over the summer. Your challenge is separating the person from you, the professional.

Start first by understanding who you are as a person. Are you interested in hobbies outside of your work? Do you have relationships with friends, significant others, or your family that do not revolve around work? Can you create a boundary between you and the persona of the classroom teacher?

Unless you are subject to an in-district residency requirement, live near but not in your district. Why? If you go shopping after work or on weekends, don't worry that an impromptu parent-teacher conference will happen while looking for your favorite cereal. You also will be asked to do a lot of extracurricular work, or you will want to watch your class members as they act in a play, sing, play in a band, or participate in athletics. Give yourself a break. It's okay to show up sometimes, but do not let the teaching world and the school become your ecosystem.

Try and schedule time for yourself weekly to de-teacher. Go out with friends away from work, but always be mindful of what you do (skip that second drink.) Take time on weekdays and weekends to meditate, engage in a hobby, or exist. Remember, adulting require you to clean, do laundry, cook, eat, and nap. We highly recommend napping.

If you are working and going to graduate school, you need to try and balance the competing requirements of both. Try hard to take only one class a semester unless you have a reason to attend school for a more intensive period. Also, consider your career goals and how graduate school will help you. With many online options, and local brick and mortar institutions, try to find a happy balance between studying and completing grad school.

A word (or a few about planning): BEG, Borrow, STEAL, utilize any pre-completed lessons from others or the publisher. Try to focus on one unit only. You must not let perfection get in the way of completion. Don't, repeat Don't get too fancy. Take some time to use the "downtime" of test proctoring or when you get paid to work on curriculum development to invest in a good lesson or unit.

A word about faculty rooms: There lie dragons. In many ways, a school faculty is often engaged in gossip, personal interplay, and overinvolvement. Try hard to keep a lot private. Share less, listen more, and spend time being present but not engaged.

Speaking of engagement: Students LOVE your personal story. They want pets, friends, significant others, everything. Students want to know about you. Use that fact to your advantage. Wear your alma mater's gear, make it an extra credit question, or weave it into your lessons. But be forewarned, do not overshare. Keep your life yours. When BIG events happen, your class can celebrate, but try hard to be human, not extra.

Events can quickly occur on social media. People are fired for what happens on social media. You MUST ensure your social media platforms are locked down tight and do not have pictures of you doing ANYTHING which may raise the hackles of the community or parent's sensibilities. Unless you are in a state with perfect laws on personal and professional rights, you are, by taxes and tuition, an employee of the school and, in some states, a public employee. Ensure that social media does not have records of youthful indiscretions, especially your unprofessional social media accounts. DO NOT UNDER ANY CIRCUMSTANCES friend your boss, your colleagues, your student's parents, or students until after they graduate, you have tenure, or you share innocuous cat memes. Albeit, you can connect with colleagues for your professional social media accounts. Overall, I suggest you keep your politics, religion, and any complaints about your boss, fellow teachers, staff, students, and families, out of the classroom and on social media. Many schools and communities are interrelated, making the world get around quickly.

Finally, have fun, enjoy life, and seek professional help if you need to, but always remember, you are you. Your career/profession/job is just that- a vehicle designed to put food on the table, a roof over your head, clothes on your back, and a mode of transport.

Activity Putting Tip #34 Into Action: Separating Your Personal Life & Career

Directions: Consider developing a plan for the following areas related to separating your personal life and career. Share your thoughts with your PLN with the hashtag **#50TeacherTipsBook**.

A Separate Life/Career Plan:	
My Goal For My Life Is:	
My Goal For My Career Is:	
What Will I Do to Separate the Two Roles:	
I Am Worried About:	
I Am Surprised About:	

Tip 35: Equity Practices & Teacher Positionality

New teachers are often pressured to be politically neutral in the classroom. It is not just scary to voice opinions inside a classroom. It can be dangerous. Stories worldwide report on teachers who have lost their job and even been sued (along with the school) for politicizing education. Equity is a taboo topic in a variety of locations.

However, schools remain a political entity. They are not and cannot be a neutral place of learning. There are many examples of power structures in play, including what curriculum is used (or not used), taught in what method, for what purpose, and to which groupings of students. Those examples only scratch the surface of a political battleground that is the foundation of any school on an international level.

The political ideologies of school and education have implications for you as an educator, whether you actively address them or not. For this book, we will only explore one implication necessary to consider from the beginning of your teaching career. We will examine its implications for your relationship with your students.

No matter how you want your school year to start, each student has preconceived notions of you, your colleagues, the school, and the entire purpose of them being in the building with you. These roles and power structures are in play before you enter the classroom and will drastically impact each student and their attitude towards you as the educator. Here are some things that each student may decide before meeting you:

- If education and their teachers are helpful or harmful to them
- The threshold of trust they are willing to give you at any point
- The respect they believe that they should give you
- The respect they expect to receive from you
- What methods of discipline will likely be enforced if they do not obey you
- How their families, friends, and role models view school
- Their self-expectations, values, beliefs, and self-image
- How many and what kind of barriers may they put up to reduce vulnerability

This list should get your mind racing with many other aspects of school that students have decided before meeting you.

Teachers cannot interact with students free from these preconceived notions and structures of power. You will likely develop solid and positive relationships with many students. But they will always be based on the foundation of their belief in your role as a teacher and their views on education as a whole.

The result of the politicized classroom is that you must consider your positionality. In other words, you must strongly understand who you are and who your students are. Well-intentioned, seemingly harmless actions can significantly harm students when you forget your positionality and fail to consider your role in the lives of your students from their perspective.

An example of harmful positionality would be a teacher who demands change from a student based on their own biases and notions of success. To push a student towards success, they may instruct that student to talk, dress, and act differently. Those lessons may be based on the teacher's experiences in their own life but may not be relevant to the student's life. The result is that the student, out of respect for a teacher their family has instructed them to trust inherently, throws away their passions and interests, which may have been the ticket to their success and happiness.

To begin working on positionality, consider your experiences and biases as a new teacher. What do you think about education? What is your view on the purpose of the curriculum? What does the perfect student act like, in your opinion? Ask and reflect on questions like these that bring biases to your mind.

As you address your own biases, you will see how they influence your conversations with your students. Coming from a position of power and authority as their teacher, your approval or rejection of their ideas and actions can potentially be life-altering. This awareness is a crucial first step in becoming a teacher who is an affirming co-learner, improving the equitable learning outcomes for and with your students.

Activity Putting Tip #35 Into Action: Evaluating Your Perspectives

Directions: Evaluate the perspectives that you bring into the classroom. Then, create an opportunity to allow your students to do the same. You can use the same questions for your students or modify them based on your class needs. This reflection is a strong starting point to an equitable classroom. Share your thoughts with your PLN with the hashtag **#50TeacherTipsBook**.

What does a K-12 school education prepare students for?	
What is the role of a teacher in a student's life?	

Tip 36: Motivation Buttons and How to Press Them

Is motivation a part of your class curriculum? Teachers often believe that motivation should come with the student. The teacher's job is to produce the specific curriculum content that students need, while the student's job is to produce the motivation necessary to complete the work. This thinking may be backward. As educators, we are not just teaching students the content, but also to think about but also how to approach the content and maximize each learning opportunity. Therefore, teaching and exemplifying motivation is critical to any teacher's classroom.

Most teachers are strong at self-motivation, yet have not thought often of how to teach a skill that seemingly comes naturally to them. Time investment in motivation training can pay huge dividends for your students' performance, though. A helpful way to approach this field is to think of motivation buttons. These are imaginary buttons that your students can press to increase their motivation towards an assignment or even schooling instantly.

To utilize motivational buttons, students need time, opportunity, and practice. This requires a profound reflection on the specific moments or elements that increase each student's level of motivation, followed by practice in implementing those cues on command. Teachers can use the following chart to begin instructing students on identifying and applying motivation buttons.

Figure 36.1

Motivation Buttons and How to Practice Them

Motivation Button	How to Practice it
Identify Role Models and the traits that make them unique, engaging, and worth wanting to emulate.	Have students write about their role models. These could be people in their life and celebrities. Get them to describe the traits they admire about those people and why they feel inspired by them.
Spotting demotivating language/word choices and replacing them with empowering phrases.	Practice evaluating word choice and phrasing as it relates to motivation. Have students check and chart how often they use phrases that cast doubt (I'm worried about, I should, I'm trying, I can't mess this up) and have them write in phrases that increase motivation instead (I'm focused on, I will, I'm going for, I'm putting effort into).

Motivation Button	How to Practice it
Visualizing success and remembering past achievements.	Have students detail moments of success, either through writing or drawing. Teach them to pay attention to the specific sensory details that made that moment special. They will pull motivation from the visual of their past accomplishments and the reminder that they are capable of greatness.
They are meeting their expectations and dropping the fear of the expectations of others.	Pair students up or have them individually work to describe the expectations they place on themselves as well as the expectations that others have placed on them. Then, work to produce statements clearly stating their self-expectations and the purpose for upholding those expectations. Finally, produce statements that analyze the expectations they believe others have for them and how they will take the positives from those expectations but be self-driven in their goals and ambitions.
Drawing motivation from outside sources.	Provide opportunities for your students to seek outside sources to filter motivation into their work consistently. This can include artwork, inspiring videos, famous quotes, biographies, documentaries, or other sources that provide motivating elements. The key to this practice is consistency. Five minutes of motivation finding per day will enable students to control and ramp up their feelings of motivation.
Intentionally applying intrinsic motivations to stay fueled.	Inward motivation is the longest-lasting and most effective form of motivation. Students should have opportunities to identify the intrinsic motivations they possess. Whether it be character traits, future job opportunities, or a positive impact they hope to create, intrinsic motivations should be clear and purposeful.

These six practices are not the only options for motivation, but they are a strong starting point. As students become more comfortable practicing motivation rather than just hoping for it, they will feel a sense of control. With practice, they will begin to self-motivate and regulate their ability to participate with more energy and attentiveness in and out of class. This is no miracle cure for your students, however. This skill, like any other, will grow with practice and deteriorate with a lack of focus. Lean into it with your class time and focus consistently, and the results will be precise.

Activity Putting Tip #36 Into Action: Motivation

Directions: Identify your motivation buttons. Review the six motivation button practices and write down what works for you. Then, plan to model yourself using those motivation buttons in front of your students. Share your thoughts with your PLN with the hashtag **#50TeacherTipsBook**.

1. Your role models:
2. Your motivating phrases:
3. Your visual when visualizing success:
4. Your personal expectations:
5. Outside sources that motivate you:
6. Your intrinsic motivation:

Tip 37: Perfection is the Enemy of Being Finished

In college, the work you submitted in class, had hard deadlines. You worked (i.e., methodically or quickly, depending on your learning and work style) on your assignments, turned the work in, and returned a grade. In some instances, you were allowed a revision opportunity. The work ended, however, as the semester ended, and you could enjoy a break. Then, next semester, you moved on to another set of classes with different expectations, assignments, and deadlines. Nothing less than an "A" grade was good enough for many. That is an admirable trait, and you will want to be the best you can be all the time.

Not so much in teaching. No matter how much your brain screams at you to "make it perfect," please do not. No matter how often your principal gives you feedback, with "next time try this method or activity," train yourself to resist the urge to redo everything to perfection. Why? You do not have time to redo everything to perfection. The professional responsibilities of a teacher are rather lengthy, and perfection can never be attained. No matter what evaluation rubrics or pundits claim, teachers, as humans, can only try to improve. As flawed human beings, we can never achieve perfection. If you try for perfection, your physical, mental, emotional, and professional health will suffer, and you will burn out.

Self-expectations from many new teachers are one of the most complex problems they face. Growing up, you went to school and saw teachers who made the "theater of teaching" look easy. How did those master practitioners create such magic? Your teachers had practice. Not every lesson was excellent. We believe that if you think through your K-12 experience as a student, you may remember when one of their lessons went poor. You didn't see the behind-the-scenes work the teacher undertook as they reflected upon what went wrong and what they would do better the next time they taught the lesson. Until you are in the trenches, you never experience the "technical" side of teaching. Like a theater production, the audience sees the result of hours of collaborative practice between the performers, the stagehands, and every support role. In teaching, you are responsible for executing teaching and learning with one significant difference: the students don't have a script or stage hand notes, and your classroom is their first classroom experience that year.

Until you have been part of the school and have repeatedly taught a grade level for a few years, you see the behind-the-scenes for the first time. Also, the world changes. In some districts, curriculum guidance is updated to meet changing standards. In New York alone, since 2001, the state has changed standards at least four times in elementary and secondary grades. Data-driven instruction is another variable added to the teaching mix. So many formative assessments, data dashboards, and teacher "gut instinct" provide a myriad of inputs to you, theoretically to help you plan, implement, evaluate and adjust instruction.

Remember that teaching is also just 180ish days. In those 180ish days, you teach from 8ish in the morning to 3ish in the afternoon. That is seven hours to accomplish English Language Arts (reading, writing, math, science, social studies, specials, lunch, breakfast, clean-up, transitions to other classrooms, and fill in the blank.

Don't forget you also have a life outside of school. You have needs and dreams and responsibilities as an adult. When you were in college, you may have started to experience this adulting if you rented an apartment. You were lucky if you lived in a dorm, ate at a cafeteria, got coffee at the student center, and focused on school. If you participated in extracurricular activities, you experienced a bit of adulting. Suppose you worked and went to school closer. If you were a non-traditional student, you probably knew what adulting is like.

So many outside influences will rear their ugly head as you start your career, and then as you progress, you will realize that there is no way to engage in perfectionism. As a professional, you are expected to grow, evolve, receive feedback, and implement the change necessary to improve your craft. At the end of the day, if you try to be perfect, you will miss the significant point: learning happens much more effectively when events fail from the established plan. Your best teaching skill will be your ability to "run with it" when the best-laid plans go sideways. Your students, who bring their own set of experiences, knowledge, and expectations, will always create opportunities to move off the established path and into the novel and new. Allow your students growth opportunities through YOUR growth opportunities. Cognitively model through wondering aloud. Yes, it's uncomfortable but so enriching.

Activity Putting Tip #37 Into Action: Perfection vs. Acceptable

Directions: Create a list of items you want to be perfect in your classroom. Now, cross it out. Make a side list of what is acceptable and does not need change. Share your thoughts with your PLN with the hashtag **#50TeacherTipsBook**.

Perfection	Acceptable

Tip 38: Theory from School Does Not Equal Practice

In college, many courses are full of theory. Starting with an introduction to psychology, we learn child and adolescent development theories. Our general courses are chocked full of theories. In sociology, we learn about society and its structure. We learn economic theories or political science ideas around civics. In history, we hear about how to interpret the past. The theory is designed to explain and organize random events and facts into an organized explanation for study. Teachers must understand the theory, but we must also implement the practice. While theory helps to explain events, remembering a crucial idea helps teachers as professionals. Every child, event, school, and family is unique and has characteristics created by their own story.

We, the authors, believe that theory is like trails in a forest. Well-worn pathways through the thickets help guide novices to their destination. The paths, tread by people in the past, often have helpful markings and signs that give hints of where to turn or a potential obstacle or hazard up ahead. But until you have experienced the trail, until you have walked the pathway yourself, and experienced the sights and smells, and sensations of the wind, mist, or the sounds of leaves rustling. The trail guideposts or signs will tell you what, in general, to do, but only experience will teach you HOW to walk along the pathway.

Experience teaches you to bring water on the trail. Why? Because you will need to quench your thirst. A guidebook will teach you to pack water, but what do you bring the water in? Do you want to carry water in a bottle? Do you want a small pack on your back called a "camelback?" Should you freeze the water ahead of time? Just like teaching, you want to have as much of your classroom ready, but the experience will teach you that on a hot day, you want frozen water, sunscreen, a floppy brimmed hat, a bandana to wipe sweat, and bug spray. Experience teaches you to wear your boots slightly before your hike and have a hiking stick, depending on the trail's grade.

Theory and research give stock, pat answers to scenarios and concerns. All the while, you are thinking, how hard can it be to create an interactive classroom student engagement policy? The theory describes how students react to motivation until they encounter a child who doesn't like the system. Then what do you do? How do you work with that child and their parents, or one set of parents who have split up, or guardians? Theory books are just that: theory. Even practical guides are only good for so much. We, the authors of this book, know that practice is the best teacher, and experience is the most excellent way to undertake an interactive career like teaching.

Experience and events will help you create your own theory as you grow personally and professionally. Your "gut instinct" and your "Spidey Sense" will grow and develop as you experience several events which will become, after a while, a trend. The trends you have experienced will grow into patterns, and then patterns begin to merge into theories. Just like hay on a farm, the accumulation of single events, like individual hay stalks, weigh little. When bundled into a hay bale, the totality can weigh a hundred pounds under the collective weight of each stalk. Thousands of hay stalks wrapped together by baling twine to form a solid object. That is how your personal experiences become theory.

Remind yourself to start with theory, but always be prepared to move beyond this starting point to practice. Most importantly, have a bag of tricks to try different strategies in your work, as your students are all unique and may not react to the "theory" presented in classes. As you grow, you will be part of professional development opportunities that may or may not provide all the answers but can give you parts. The best learning often happens when something does not work well the first time. We all learn and grow from reflection, so keep trying, never give up, and never surrender.

Activity Putting Tip #38 Into Action: Theory and Practice

Directions: Name a theory and then name a practice. Limit it to five. How will you implement it in the classroom? Share your thoughts with your PLN with the hashtag **#50TeacherTipsBook**.

Activity: What Theory?	What Practice?

Tip 39: Food is Critical to You and Your Students

There is an expression that teachers drink coffee for others' protection. Caffeine is valuable to an educator's diet, but you must eat right. As you move along in your day, week, month, and career, you will have changing needs from a dietary perspective. But rule number 1 needs to remain written in stone: feed yourself healthy foods.

Rule number one for students: always assume they are hungry. We cannot tell you how far food goes with students. Some students may not have eaten healthy, or enough. Far too often, carbs become the go-to for taste or convenience, and sugar seems everywhere in a student's diet. Our poor students, who depend on school food, may eat sugary breakfast cereal and have a starch-laden lunch. No wonder the kids are falling asleep. Their glycemic index is up and down.

Far too often, teachers will eat school food, and having access to vending machines makes unwise choices about what to consume. While your teens and twenties meant fast food or caffeinated sugary drinks, your body will inform you that you made poor choices as you age. Make sure you try to balance your food at work and home. Your food needs to be enjoyed, so don't scarf. That means hold your lunch period sacred and try hard to eat during lunch. Relax, enjoy, and be calm. If you choose to, you can use lunch as a reward for excellent work on something.

I have also found providing food for your class an excellent strategy to help engagement, encourage camaraderie, and often relieve hunger. With the number of allergies and safety restrictions, please discuss with your mentor, union, or school administrator first. Have, if possible, use PTA grants or donations, and snacks in the classroom, if allowed to. A student may appreciate a granola bar if they skip breakfast. Or a student might appreciate the apples or raisins. You could discuss a class pizza party or make your own sandwich party for a class opportunity to get to know each other.

Be aware of any medical restrictions students or others have. Diabetes is a disease that restricts students from eating sweets. Allergies are the worst, and the most common are nuts and wheat.

You can also build food into your lessons. In one of Casey's social studies classes, I asked students to compare and contrast fruits and grains originating in the western hemisphere with eastern foods. I asked students to look at how the food products originated, were cultivated, and became part of the interhemispheric exchange (Jakubowski, 2020). I had students examine how the environment impacted different communities' cultures and social norms. At the time, students in a rural area of Upstate New York had not experienced mangos, star fruit, and other fruits that are now commonplace and part of our smoothie regimes. In several urban and rural communities, students have not experienced different food varieties and would benefit from an organized cultural event highlighting diversity and commonality.

Be aware of religious and cultural restrictions. During the lesson, one of my students was participating in a Ramadan fast, so I ensured that I sent the food home with him so that he could enjoy it after sundown. I also want teachers to know our major religious communities' restrictions. Please take time, and do a little reading about what observant members can eat and can't. For instance, both adherents to Judaism and Islam will not eat pork, so be sure nothing in the food is pork-related (oil used to fry potato chips is one hidden example). For some observant Buddhists and Sikhs, avoiding animal-based products is a requirement. Some googling or conversations with students or their parents can be helpful.

In summary, be aware of your dietary needs and your student's needs, and ensure you remember this: a hungry student is a distracted student. Ensure students are getting food and offer snacks to build communities. Never be afraid to speak to a guidance counselor, mentor, or administrator if you are concerned about a student. Try to eat well, and be aware that stress and the rhythm and flow of the year can tempt you. Last, your lunchtime should be used for lunch only.

Activity Putting Tip #39 Into Action: Plan a Food and Beverage Policy Menu

Directions: Create a plan for food and beverages in your classroom. Share your thoughts with your PLN with the hashtag **#50TeacherTipsBook**.

Tip 40: Restorative Justice

According to We Are Teachers (2021), "Restorative justice is a theory of justice that focuses on mediation and agreement rather than punishment. Offenders must accept responsibility for harm and make restitution to victims." Restorative practice is rooted in Indigenous practices. Restorative practices build school communities and respectfully address challenges caused by challenging behavior. Instead of punishing students, these practices promote restoring relationships among students and a student taking ownership of their behaviors. Restorative practices improve the school climate in many ways, including:

- Reducing in and out of school suspensions and office referrals
- Creating a classroom community through circles
- Ensuring students are heard and valued
- Strengthen social and emotional skills
- Strengthen relationships within the classroom.
- Promoting trust with the teacher and peers
- Improving inclusive practices
- Resolving Conflict
- Permitting students advocate for themselves and others

Restorative practices range from low-level classroom conversations to more structured conversations. Restorative practices comprise a continuum of intervention. These strategies can be used daily or weekly or when a tragedy occurs in the community or school. According to We Are Teachers (2021), there are three tiers of restorative justice. The first tier focuses on prevention through building community.

In Tier I educators lead conversation circles where students can share their feelings, discuss topics or use a social-emotional check-in with students. Students feel valued and supported in this tier. They work to build trust among themselves and their teachers. In this tier, the class develops a classroom respect agreement. This agreement holds all students accountable (We are Teachers, 2021).

Tier II occurs if a student breaks a rule or causes harm to a peer. Restorative justice provides the student with the opportunity to make amends. When this occurs, a teacher mediates conversations with those involved in the incident (We Are Teachers, 2021). In this tier, the teacher must use non-judgment questions to get to the bottom of the situation.

Reintegration into the school community is the focus of Tier III. This reintegration can be due to an in or out-of-school suspension, school expulsion, or other removals of a student from the classroom. In this tier, the team must recognize that students may struggle with reintegrating into the classroom community (We are Teachers, 2021).

How to get started with restorative practices

- Know your biases
- Use affective and effective language with students during practice
- Student check-ins

For more information about restorative practices

- https://restorativejustice.org/what-is-restorative-justice/
- https://www.iirp.edu/news/restorative-practices-shows-promise-for-meeting-new-national-school-discipline-guidelines
- https://www.edutopia.org/blog/restorative-justice-resources-matt-davis

Putting Tip #40 Into Action: Reviewing Restorative Practice Resources

Directions: Review the resources listed above for more ideas about how to implement restorative practices in the classroom. Jot down your ideas below and discuss how they can be implemented in your classroom. Share your thoughts with your PLN with the hashtag **#50TeacherTipsBook**.

Critical Conversation Three: Working through a Tragedy on Campus - How to Navigate Tragedy and How to Support the School Community as a Teacher

Casey shares: In elementary school, a tragedy struck. One of the girls died in a fire set by her father. In memory, our school went outside, where a tree planting and remembrance ceremony brought more questions to mind: Who was she? How did she die? The teachers didn't want to tell us much beyond it being a tragedy. Having lived through the experience of my little brother dying, I guess my brain engaged slightly differently than other children. As I grew older, my grandparents passed away, and it was sad. I lost a friend just after I graduated from school and openly wept with his mother. But when a student or a colleague dies, it hits differently. We all must live with death and mourn based on cultural or religious traditions. When a student dies, the impact on the adults, the community, and our children are so profound.

During the summer of 2004, a car accident between teenage drivers and passengers resulted in the death of one of our juniors. One of our former students, Army Specialist Isaac Nieves, died in Iraq by experiencing an Improvised Explosive Device (IED) in April of 2004. Our community's reaction, in a tiny little village in Southern Tier New York, was one of public mourning, along with the private grief of his family. A school memorial service included the choir, his family, and his brother (a Cadet at West Point) to mourn Isaac's loss. Later that week, one of my students, Natasha, died by suicide. As the community came together for her very public funeral, a parent of another one of my students died in a car accident on the way to a second memorial service. It was as if God had decided our village deserved to face the wrath of immense power and destructiveness. As the faculty and staff, we cried at home; we mourned in an attempt to try not only to honor our students, alums, and parents but each other.

The superintendent called a two-hour delay for our students, and we met that morning with a grief professional. I remember her words: I cannot believe how you are all dealing with three traumatic incidents. I sat there thinking, *I need my mom and dad. I want to go home.* We had not had our spring break yet and were emotionally exhausted from just the regular spring. I needed to go home and cry. So over spring break I went home, and they cried with me. Two deaths were accidental, while Isaac's death was the result of a policy. Natasha's death was so hard. What had I not done? What should I have done to be there for her and prevent the overwhelming hurt?

As Casey moved on in his career and went to work for State Education, a student's death occurred at one of the schools the Department oversaw in all areas of operations: academic, financial, structural, and security. That day, I had just explained to the high school principal and the superintendent the metal detectors were malfunctioning in the building. When I left the district and was heading back to Albany, I heard on the radio that a student was stabbed to death on the playing fields. I pulled over and called my supervisor, who asked questions, and took down facts. I received at least two phone calls on that three-hour drive. And once again, the questions rose: What could I have done? What should I have done? Why, God, Why? The next day, on my drive to my parent's home for Easter, I spent at least three phone calls with my supervisor, reporting more facts and helping develop an action plan. For three days, I typed up a report, a letter of transmittal, and a corrective action plan for my supervisor to sign and send to the district immediately. We were documenting what WE had done and would do to support and oversee the district as a family mourning.

In Casey's role on Rochester, NY's administrative team, we suffered a student's death. I called the principal of the school to offer my condolences and sympathies. She wept on the phone because every one of her students was hers, and she felt so much pain because one of her babies was gone, taken by senseless reasons on the streets. What haunts me to this day, though, is the suicide of a colleague who faced job elimination long after I was gone from her life. She wanted to be, and was by and far, one of the MOST dedicated, creative, and student-centered educators I have ever met. Her death hit me hard. While we will never know why she died of suicide, her job loss and the inexcusable way the district eliminated positions must have had an impact.

As I write this piece, the COVID-19 pandemic is over a year and one-half old. Teachers, students, parents, grandparents, and loved ones are dying. Almost every place has experienced death from the pandemic. And almost every place has been touched, in some way, by loss from war, hatred, rage, disease, or accident. I do not honestly know what to tell you to do if death visits your school. I believe in a higher power, but besides praying, I cannot tell you what more to do. Yes, counseling helps. Yes, seeking medical assistance helps. But at the end of the day, all you can do is mourn. Create a safe space in your classroom for your kids because death is one of those huge issues, and academics can stuff a pepper. I am in no way an expert on what to do, but I will tell you this, I remember every single person I have lost.

Rest in Peace, Sarah, Isaac, Tash, Mr. K. RC, and Mrs. P. You are loved, you are valued, and you are remembered.

Below is the author team's dialogue around dealing with tragedy in critical conversation three.

Matt: After reading about Casey's experiences with school tragedies, we will dive deep and discuss how to further navigate these harrowing experiences of tragedy and loss within our school community. These tragedies can include students or colleagues, or personally. These tragedies can include trauma outside or inside the school, including death, illness, bullying, divorce, breakup, or financial hardship. Micro and macro traumas can result from these tragedies, which can build over time. Our goal of this discussion is to outline various types of support, including focusing on mental healthcare and services offered within our school community that can support not only ourselves as teachers but also our colleagues and students to create a sense of community in the workplace. I will open it up to the rest of us to discuss how we can navigate tragedy, whether it is personal, within the school community, and what we can do in terms of providing tips and strategies to navigate it ourselves and being there for our students.

Kevin: So when I've dealt with tragedies in school, one thing I've learned is to be the person who validates the experience of her students rather than dismissing them. And, I've seen that a lot. There are various types of tragedies, where some students might feel outraged, some may feel guilty, and they're going through those different stages of grief or processing their trauma. It's straightforward as a teacher when you're, you know, busy in your day to just get caught up in the solution-oriented don't think that think this instead of trying to correct them and in their thinking. It's essential to allow them to experience what they're feeling rather than shutting it out, especially not being mental health experts and just being the person in the classroom - it's vital to stay in that position of being validating and understanding to others. It's also important to recognize your feelings.

Sam: Our feelings are paramount and critical when working through the trauma. I support students by giving them grace, giving them time to process, and giving myself time to process and grieve All of these factors will help you in the long run by not rushing through the grieving process, and knowing that the process doesn't have a timeline and can pop up at any time is essential to consider when a tragedy strikes.

Casey: I have profoundly and personally experienced tragedy in my teaching career where there was a direct loss of students I knew at my school. When tragedy strikes, let's not forget that the community engages daily with people having their tragedies as well as external tragedies. A book out there called Teaching the Day After by Alyssa Dunn helps us understand that we are first to spend time making sure we are okay. Then secondly, make sure your students are okay. I would venture to say that we need to be most concerned about the rise in people experiencing trauma at the end of the day. So, I think that when we experience tragedy, we must remember that trauma comes along with it. As a result, we must seek help on trauma-informed teaching, resources to provide a place of grace and space for our students, and stop and think about the most crucial part of teaching, which is not to cover the content. But it is to teach the students how to be community members.

Matt: The notion of community is fundamental, especially when tragedy strikes. In my experience, I've not necessarily had students I directly worked with die. Still, we had several situations where we've experienced trauma due to a lockdown or bomb threat. Due to these traumatizing scenarios, the local community and school community helped support students and teachers by providing opportunities for counselors and service animals to come onto campus to help begin the healing process.

As teachers, we should be open about mental health in our classes. Teachers need to be the first line of defense to not stigmatize going to a therapist. Additionally, we need to normalize it okay for educators and students alike to see a therapist - working on our mental health is like going to the gym as it helps create a healthy rhythm in your life. It is essential teachers know how to navigate mental health services and providers because it's crucial teachers have the ability, resources, and the yearning to see a therapist as they experience individual and collective trauma in their daily work teaching and leading.

Teachers must find a supportive group of educators and individuals outside of education, such as friends and family, that they can converse with regarding what you're going through every day. This is critical as it allows teachers to discuss and process events that unfolded. Finally, I believe that if you're able to model, you have a strong support network with students that gives them a good insight into how to navigate difficult circumstances, including tragedy.

Casey: I believe one of the areas that we forget in education is Maslow before Bloom. It represents, in many ways, new thinking, but it shouldn't be new. It should be ingrained in our rituals and routines. It needs to focus on activating resources beyond therapy dogs and the generalized support we see when tragedy strikes. Schools and administrators need to implement ongoing support in our classrooms and schools that represent Maslow before Bloom, which is our student's well-being above all else before we can focus on improving their academic skills.

New teachers need to practice Maslow before Bloom and remember what didn't work well and what they can do personally and professionally to improve their practices in this regard. I think seeking guidance from senior teachers can help a little, but a peer support group will help even more. It's also important to note that we are all on our journey, and while others may be ready to implement a new practice, we can take our time as it may not be the right time for our students, or we are ready.

In sum, in processing a tragedy, you must personally go through the grieving process. You only have your students in class with you for 185 days, but you have to recognize that tragedy and coping with strategy can come at an unexpected time. Be aware of this and be prepared to navigate it personally and with your students in your class.

Sam: Having a peer support group is essential. I think finding colleagues who have gone through similar traumas or experiences is helpful—finding common ground with colleagues and supporting each other, whether sharing how you're feeling or spending time together. Finding colleagues that can help support you and having a peer support group can be helpful during times of tragedy.

In addition to all the other mentioned strategies, let us look into new teachers. Like all campuses, there will be several new teachers. While having support groups of new and experienced teachers is essential, there are outlets new teachers can utilize to discuss important issues and experiences together. Within your school, district, and maybe even finding a peer support group online, whether that's any groups on social media online through a professional learning network.

Kevin: I love using online resources because it allows you to connect to teachers who aren't in your specific context but have gone through similar tragedies or traumas. A lot of this is that not everything works the same way for the same person.

So when you go online, and you go to a place like Twitter, and you reach out to teachers by posting, "Have you ever faced this situation before?" it can be beneficial to get a range of perspectives to see. When you read the response, you think about how you may not think of that idea, or maybe that one would help me more than what I was trying myself. Maybe it's something I didn't even think about, or maybe they can point you to a resource that people within your school community have never heard of, so those online connections are critical, like Sam said. I'd also add tapping into community resources and parents.

One thing that has helped me a lot while navigating different types of traumas in school is to reach out to people in the community. Who else knows the family as well? Who knows the situations better than I do, in the context behind everything that has happened or is currently happening? Having that kind of support system gives you people outside your school setting. Overall, having a local support network of teachers who are teaching with you on a day-to-day basis but are familiar with the people involved in the things that are happening is critical. They can give you guidance and a supportive community that isn't necessarily about education but healing from that trauma.

Matt: It's a team effort when it comes down to it while navigating tragedy and trauma. Working with students, school administration, and the support staff comes down to group effort and coordination. As a teacher in the classroom, you can help facilitate that with those team members. The best analogy is that you're the facilitator - the point guard. You can also be the person they can have the opportunity to speak with about, as well as all the different team members to have that conversation with you and point them in the right direction. Ultimately, what it comes down to is the team effort. With that team effort, the school community can help steer students in the right direction to receive the support and services they need to process trauma and navigate tragedy. All of this comes down to communication. Be very open in terms of communication channels. Follow up and describe what's happening, but also be aware of student privacy and know this information should only be shared with key stakeholders and service providers.

Final Thoughts - Critical Conversation #3

Throughout this conversation, we've talked about several strategies and resources to help navigate tragedy in our classrooms and schools, from the personal level of the teacher to supporting students and accessing the school community and support network. We hope these experiences and strategies help you navigate these situations. It is guaranteed you will experience tragedy and trauma in your career in education. Therefore, it is essential to have a foundation of knowledge and experiences to help you navigate them as best as possible - remember, you're not going to be perfect. It's okay to ask for help. It's okay to be a teammate through these circumstances because they're not meant to be circumstances for you to navigate alone. Ultimately, it's a community effort, and our goal should be to continue to build community every day so that when tragedy and trauma do strike, there's a community of support there for educators and students alike to help them process and navigate the circumstance.

SECTION 4: ARE WE THERE YET?

April   May

June

"Celebrate. Learn. Enjoy. Win. Innovate, Create. Rest. Learn. Dream. Love. Do. Be". - Robin Sharma

Section 4: Are We There Yet?

It's spring. This is the most significant part of the school year as the snow melts, the temperatures rise, and the students (and teachers) become restless. Some of you are fresh off of a spring break trip. Some of you may start hearing one of your colleagues is engaged, expecting, or switching jobs. Yes, it's that time of the year. The last three months of school change from districts planning for next year to teachers planning their next career, family, or real estate move. You may be asked about what assignment you would like for next year. Your grad classes are wrapping up, so projects need to be done, or a major thesis is due. Your mind will be in three places: The present, the future, and the anticipation of summer vacation: practice recentering yourself and your class. If possible, find ways to utilize the great outdoors for lessons. Begin collaborating with people who you want to work with on summer projects. Plan for the mad dash at the end of June, and please give yourself time to rest. YOU NEED IT!

Tips and Strategy Entries 41-50

Tip 41: Navigating the Present and Future of Education The Learning Management System is Key

The learning management system (LMS) is the central hub where content, instruction, and communication are distributed and facilitated in modern classrooms. Teachers use LMS as an airport where students can use its various runways to interact with the digital content used for the class. Additionally, an LMS provides teachers and students a hub where instruction and content can be accessed at any time once it's been uploaded and updated. Ultimately, this allows students to access instruction and content anywhere and anytime inside and outside the four walls of their physical classroom.

Using an LMS with an assortment of EdTech tools allows you to provide instruction anywhere and anytime. The goal is to demonstrate how an LMS is a foundation for this infrastructure and an opportunity to provide more equity and continuous learning for your students. Then, tips and tricks will be given regarding how to use LMSs effectively and deliver instruction efficiently from them.

You've Used One Before

In all likelihood, you have used an LMS before as a student. As a student, you may have had to navigate many LMSs. You may have used one or more of the LMSs currently being deployed in classrooms as a teacher. Many LMSs you may encounter include Google Classroom, Canvas, Blackboard, Schoology, and Seesaw, which take up the bulk of the market. Based on what you've experienced, several characteristics may make it easier or more challenging to navigate or utilize in your practice. Let's explore a few of these characteristics.

1. **Organization -** An organized LMS involves easy-to-navigate buttons, accessible content, and content chunked into daily, weekly, or unit-based work.
2. **Tasks and Assignments are Clear -** A high-quality built-out LMS provides opportunities for teachers to share instructions and add media to enhance the instructions provided.
3. **Teacher Feedback is Accessible -** Teacher feedback is critical within an LMS. They will provide feedback to the entire class through a whole class announcement or directly onto student work. When students can easily access feedback, they will interact more with the LMS.

Overall, by now, you've probably seen and experienced your fair share of LMSs in your experience in education. You've seen which ones you thought were effective versus ones in classes that were not. To ensure your future use of an LMS is successful, try each of these three characteristics in the one you will deploy. It does not have to be extravagant. Please keep it simple. Stay consistent. Then, adjust as needed based on student needs and their experience.

Why? Equity and Continuous Learning

An LMS is a foundational piece to allow for learning to be continuous for your students. For example, students can complete tasks and assignments in class. Then, students can access those same tasks and assignments for instructions and even recorded class segments to help them activate their prior knowledge. Additionally, resources that allow students to practice what they've learned can be integrated directly into the LMS. This provides students the opportunity to practice and refine their skills. Last, a teacher can communicate with students and families and easily showcase and share their student's work with stakeholders. Doing this allows everyone involved in a child's education to see how the student is doing and how they can further support the student.

These opportunities enhance the student's learning experience by taking parts of the classroom anywhere. In addition, students can access their materials, resources, and assignments. When a device and internet connection are available to students and their LMS, it creates a far more equitable learning opportunity than what was available in the past. Now, students can essentially review and even conduct the lesson in class and continue receiving many of the same supports and resources at any time. For example, if they need to rewatch content on a video or pause the video as the teacher works out a problem, they can solve it. This format provides flexibility in the student's ability to work at their own pace and at their own time.

Tips for Utilizing an LMS as a Teacher

Let's review five tips for utilizing an LMS while teaching a class. Ultimately, the goal is to create an LMS where your teaching style can shine. Additionally, we want our students to have access to access and navigate content easily. Last, we want to do this as efficiently as possible as we know our time is finite. Therefore, each of these five tips considers this. You aim to create systems around implementing each tip into your practice that best suits your workflow.

- **Buildout Your Content a Week in Advance -** Each week, you want to have the main content of your lessons posted on your LMS. This can include an outline of static hyperlinks added daily or having everything fully added first thing on Monday morning. This provides a framework for your class's schedule for the week. Also, we can focus on providing feedback and planning out the following week. It can be adjusted as needed, but the goal is to have it built out as it will ultimately save you time.
- **Create a Majority of Classroom Routines around the LMS -** When students access the LMS, routines must be developed so that students can complete assignments and tasks, consume content, and access resources and supports. Creating routines on the first day of school and building them up over the next few weeks around everything you do with your LMS will go a long way. Throughout the year, you will have to revisit and practice these routines. You may even add or subtract a few routines here and there. However, with an LMS being front and center in your classroom, routines to use, navigate, and complete tasks will be the pinnacle for your student's success.
- **Record Every Time You Model and Provide Direct Instruction -** When you are modeling and using instruction, especially on your computer screen projected to the class, record those lesson segments and upload them to your LMS. Using a platform like Loom, you can easily record segments of your lesson so students can review them at any time after the lesson has been completed. Try to keep the recordings short. Chunking them into three to five-minute clips is an excellent time to allow students to process the instruction.
- **Provide Feedback on the LMS, But Not Too Much -** Provide feedback to your students by analyzing trends through whole class communication and then speak to your students for individualized feedback. Doing this through an LMS is to provide your critical feedback in a communication sent to the entire class and discussed during your synchronous instruction. Once this whole class feedback has been provided, you can focus on students you want to provide more individualized feedback by commenting on their assignments in the LMS and meeting with them in person.
- **Organization - Less is More -** When using an LMS, we want to keep it organized and easy to navigate. We want to think less is more in what we publish and provide on our LMS. The fewer clicks and pages students have to visit and navigate, the better. We aim to make it as accessible as possible for our students, and we do not want them to get lost or overwhelmed.

123

Conclusion - An LMS is Your Central Hub

An LMS is your central hub that will continue to be one of the main places where you distribute content, facilitate instruction, and communicate with your students and their families. There is no doubt the LMS will evolve and change over time. Yet, it is a cornerstone of modern classrooms where you can provide opportunities for your students to learn within and outside the classroom walls. Hopefully, the information provided here can help you refine and build your skills in using one. Ultimately, think less is more and develop classroom routines that support its use. It will go a long way in making a practical part of your classroom and something that will not be a burden to continue updating and utilizing to create equitable learning opportunities.

Activity Putting Tip #41 Into Action: 3 Themes, 2 Things to Do, 1 Question or Extension

Directions: Write down three significant themes you were able to gather from this tip. Then, describe two things you will do with your LMS to amplify how you use it further. Third, write down a question you may have or an area you would like to learn more about related to the content discussed in this tip. How can you get this question answered? Share your thoughts with your PLN with the hashtag **#50TeacherTipsBook**.

3 Themes	2 Things to Do	1 Question or Extension

Tip 42: The Burnout Cycle

Many professionals view burnout as a yes or no question. "Are you burned out?" they may ask with good intentions. Unfortunately, the research does not offer the same clarity on burnout. It is not a syndrome that comes and goes as it pleases. Burnout is a cycle that traps workers (often in service fields) and spins them through varying degrees of symptoms and challenges. For teachers, understanding the burnout cycle can save years of stress, heartache, and the ability to remain unharmed in their careers.

Kevin began his dissertation research to understand the burnout process for new teachers. It shocked him to learn that the teachers who were most likely to burn out were educators in the first five years of the profession. Media had led him to believe that burnout was for older, experienced teachers. In his pursuit of answers, he found many trends leading to the New Teacher Cycle of Burnout (Leichtman, 2019).

Figure 42.1

The New Teacher Burnout Cycle

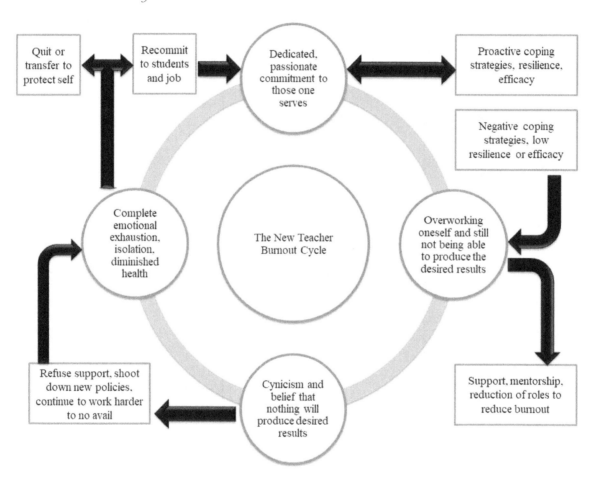

Stage 1: Passion

Burnout begins when a person is passionately committed to their profession. Lacking passion, burnout does not exist. Apathy takes its place. As teachers enter the profession full of a desire to impact education and shape the minds of young students, weight begins to pull at them. They seek the best results and best effort from themselves to fulfill their passion. This constant drive must battle their desires outside the classroom and balance other aspects of their lives (friends, family, spouses, hobbies, financial responsibilities, etc.).

Stage 2: Overwork

The cycle continues as a person's commitment leads to overworking and overwhelming yourself. People passionate about their job will give their all to make the most significant and enduring impact possible. This burnout often leads to planning, grading, and feedback given outside of contractual hours for teachers. It also includes volunteering at the school, attending sporting events, and hosting clubs. The constant drive to be a great teacher can quickly make you feel overworked and can never catch up to all of your tasks.

Stage 3: Cynicism

What happens when you overwork yourself and do not receive the desired results? We give ourselves to the career, only to see more responsibilities added, more challenges placed in front of us, and more data points and accountability measures to hit. The constant overwork and lack of payoff (neither financially nor emotionally rewarding) may quickly lead to a negative feeling. Burnout becomes intense when you feel that there will be no improvement at your job. You keep pouring yourself into it, but you believe that the job will never give you back satisfaction. You may become cynical about policies, programs, and professional development opportunities.

Stage 4: Complete Exhaustion

Burnout can be an all-encompassing stressor. Cynicism and a constant feeling of overwhelm will eventually result in complete exhaustion. As each burnout cycle completes, physical and emotional issues will grow in strength. By this point, a teacher may be completely isolated, depressed, and lacking purpose or joy. This powerful, draining feeling does not remain at work. It follows them home and everywhere they go. A teacher's decision marks this final stage of the cycle: quit or recommit.

Beating burnout starts with understanding the cycle it will take you through. Identify where you are on the cycle right now. What feelings are dominating your work day? The goal is not to avoid the burnout cycle but to constantly maintain stage one. Feed your passion for the profession, but be careful that it does not lead you to overwhelm.

Activity Putting Tip #42 Into Action: The Burnout Cycle

Directions: Determine where you are in the burnout cycle currently. Come up with a plan to reset and return to a point where you are passionate, but before feeling overwhelmed. Share your thoughts with your PLN with the hashtag **#50TeacherTipsBook**.

What stage of the burnout cycle am I in currently?
What two actions can I apply daily to reduce my feelings of burnout?
Who can I go to within my school to help me process and overcome feelings of burnout?
Who / what resources can I go to outside of my school to reduce my feelings of burnout?

Tip 43: Bringing in Local and World-Renowned Experts into Your Classroom

In the book *The Expert Effect*, McKinney and Rondot (2021) discuss how experts can join classrooms and teach students about their expertise relating to the content and skills. Ultimately, our students need to see the content and skills in practice. Increasing the relevancy of what our students are learning will increase their engagement and illustrate connections we can make to what we are learning to how individuals and industries are changing our local and global communities. The goal is to provide a summarized framework for bringing experts into your class to amplify the relevancy of the content and skills you teach your students.

How to Bring in Experts

Bringing in local and global experts sounds like quite a bit of extra work while planning a unit of study. However, in our world today, experts do not need to visit your classroom physically. Additionally, this outreach could result in much more engaged learners who have a future interest in that profession. To facilitate this in your classroom, a three-step framework provided below includes

- Recruiting experts.
- Utilizing technology to bring them in.
- Integrating the visit into your unit of study.

Recruiting. Recruiting may seem daunting. Rejection by the expert may seem inevitable because it is. Unfortunately, it is a numbers game at first. However, with time, effort, and focus on building relationships, this numbers game can turn into a network of experts willing to jump into your classroom from time to time to present and meet with your students.

Use LinkedIn and company websites to learn more about the person. Additionally, research industry journals or online communities to further identify individuals. Also, see if current student family members, school alumni or business and community partnerships can be utilized to find and identify experts. Once an individual is identified, you must determine if their expertise meets your curriculum and learning objectives for the unit you teach. As outlined before, continue researching their industry and individual(s) expertise. Then, before reaching out, compile a list of individuals you may want to contact. Also, be sure you have the permissions from your school's admin team and the school's protocols ready when someone accepts. Then, develop a form email letter that you will send, including information about your school and classroom. You will send the first email to your top three expert guests.

As you start sending out emails, start with three individuals. Send the emails to them at least a month out before the unit begins and give them a set of days within the next unit of study where they could attend class. If you do not get a response during the first week, send out another set of emails to the following two experts on your list, and then send three emails to the first three experts as reminders about the proposal to attend a class you recently sent. Ultimately, it is a numbers game, and plan for an alternate activity if you cannot recruit an expert to jump into class virtually or in person.

Best Way to Use Technology to Bring Them In. We now have the opportunity to bring in experts using a virtual meet platform. We have Google Meet, Zoom, Microsoft Teams, and Skype for a live synchronous meeting. We can also have the interaction recorded early on via Meet, Zoom, Teams, or an application like Loom, Screencastify, or StreamYard. Beyond the video, if the expert brings in a slideshow, you can create opportunities for active engagement by using Pear Deck or Nearpod to make the slideshow interactive. You can ask experts if they have a slideshow they will present. If they do, ask for it beforehand to review and make it interactive and engaging for your students. You can add formative assessment and check for understanding opportunities and active learning engagement strategies to amplify the lesson and activity. One last thing to take note of is to set the tone for your speaker when they are invited to your class. Within the email, outline various engagement strategies to meet your student's needs so that the speaker makes their slideshow or presentation materials with that in mind from the start.

Activities for Students. Take the content and resources from the expert to connect their visit to the curriculum and amplify what you have taught in class. Beyond ensuring the slideshow is engaging, teachers can plan several activities like WebQuests, virtual field trips, evidence-gathering tasks, short-response questions, and summarization and self-reflection. Ultimately, these activities are the tip of the iceberg as we want them to align with the expert's visit and the learning objectives for the lesson and unit of study.

We live in a world more connected than ever before. This means we can discover, vet, and invite experts into our classroom that can amplify our classroom. Having a local or global expert share their content and role in a specific topic allows our students a deeper look into that industry or topic. It may provoke a student's interest to investigate further. It also may motivate a student to want to pursue a career in the expert industry.

Now more than ever, thanks to our connections and technology, we can make this possible. As a result, having an expert come into class may be life-changing for our students. Therefore, it makes all the effort to recruit and bring experts into the classrooms worth it.

Activity Putting Tip #43 Into Action: Getting Experts into Your Classroom

Directions: Consider how bringing an expert into your class can help amplify what the students are learning. Break down several upcoming units you will be teaching. What type(s) of experts could you bring into your class? Then, discuss how they can fit into the unit and content you are teaching your students. Share your thoughts with your PLN with the hashtag **#50TeacherTipsBook**.

Unit:	Unit:	Unit:	Unit:
Possible Experts 1. 2. 3	**Possible Experts** 1. 2. 3	**Possible Experts** 1. 2. 3	**Possible Experts** 1. 2. 3
How can the expert fit into the unit?	**How can the expert fit into the unit?**	**How can the expert fit into the unit?**	**How can the expert fit into the unit?**

Tip 44: Student Reflections for the Year End

Reflections are one of the most powerful learning opportunities a school year provides. They can also be the most crippling learning experiences. A year of school comes with its share of success and barriers to success for any student. Rather than ignoring the ups and downs, it is helpful to help students navigate them. Even a school year full of negatives can lead to a positive reflection and an experiential learning experience.

Have students reflect on their year by focusing on strengths, growth, and continuous improvement opportunities. Similar to an athletic coach, hammering weaknesses will only highlight them. Those weaknesses can drain the confidence and motivation out of your students and sap their progress in the coming years. Reflections can acknowledge their difficulties with a forward-focused lens that helps them fine-tune and improve their approach. Remember, the objective is to utilize a student's assets and abilities to create momentum.

Activity Putting Tip #44 Into Action: Reflection Chart

Directions: Here is a reflection chart that Matt has used throughout his years in education. He has edited it many times and probably will continue to. Feel free to incorporate it into your class and adjust it to the needs of your students. Keep the reflection goals in mind as you roll this out towards the end of the school year. Share your thoughts with your PLN with the hashtag **#50TeacherTipsBook**.

Prompt	Student Response
What character trait do you believe is your strongest? Write a time when you showed it.	
What character trait did you improve on the most this year? How did you see that happen?	

Prompt	Student Response
When did you feel most successful this year? (In or out of school) Why?	
When did you feel most challenged this year? (In or out of school) How did you overcome that challenge?	
Were there any challenges that you have not yet overcome? What is your plan to continue working on it?	
What trait or skill will you work on over the summer to continue growing as a student and as a person?	

Prompt	Student Response
What hobby or passion will give you more time, attention, and energy?	
What positive phrase or affirmation can you say to remind yourself of the person you want to become?	

Tip 45: The Faculty Room… Sigh

As students in school, did you ever wonder what happened behind the faculty room door? That magic portal, leading from the shared space of the school into the private world of the teachers, creates a space of exclusion. As student teachers, we entered the faculty room timidly, sometimes told to be seen and not heard. The faculty room held a refrigerator for lunches (when remembered), a microwave, and a food and soft drink vending machine. In most professional's opinion, the essential part of the faculty room was the coffee pot. In the days before laptops, desktop computers and printers provided a workspace for traveling teachers who had no room of their own.

During the day, teachers without a homeroom, a duty, or a classroom would wander down. Some would eat, others would correct work, but mostly they talked and drank caffeine. On "appreciation days," bagels, donuts, or entire meals appeared, and often before the winter holiday break, a potluck was organized by our union to celebrate our break from the kids, stress, and work. The room had no windows and did not have attached bathrooms. The nearest adult bathroom was outside, in the hallways, on the left of the door. It was a small corner of the school, surrounded by the nurse, the high school office, and the band storage room. When no one was there, it became a place of refuge for faculty trying to prepare for their next class or catch up from the morning's classes. Notifications about upcoming opportunities or newsletters found their way into the faculty room. In the early 2000s, most materials were mailed, printed, and physically handed about. The room became the touch point to buy lottery tickets, as we hoped for a big win, the March Madness pools, or the sales for clubs and organizations.

One pattern you begin to notice is who sits where and doesn't come to the faculty room. There are cliques among school staff, and some stay away from others. Some faculty rooms had pretty mean people, who often verbally dismissed others for "caring too much" or "trying too hard." You may notice terrific teachers stay out of the faculty room and choose to avoid the blackhole of outer space. These teachers would move around to other rooms if their classrooms were in use. They would do their work in other people's classrooms. They never went to the faculty room. They wanted nothing to do with the people there and what those people represented.

As a novice teacher, always remember to pay for the coffee club unless you do not drink coffee. Remember: your workplace is not your life. It is a big part but should not be the be-all and end-all. You need to ensure that you do not transfer to the people in the faculty room any more than your professionalism.

Never talk about another faculty, staff, administrator, student, family, or anyone from the community in the faculty lounge. The walls have ears, and other teachers won't keep your opinions confidential if they use gossip as a way to enrich their status. Use materials or space in the faculty room but seek guidance from trusted folks away from the school community. Be very careful about picking up and taking everything with you when you leave the room. Piles of paper are gold mines for comparisons and snoopers. Always remember that student work and files are private and should not be left in the room. Also, remember that you should not do school work on a personal computer, and you really should not use school equipment or programs to access home or personal information. Find positive, like-minded people. Be careful of gossip, and be aware of how you frame what you say and do in the faculty room. You may be lucky and find support and collegiality, but be aware of the realities of what happens in your school, especially in informal places.

Lastly, don't feel pressured to buy everything students sell in a school. Remember, your first five years are costly with little salary and many expenses. Focus on what groups you advise, want to advise, or believe are critical to support. Donate a dollar if you want to help, but the products may be too expensive. I wish you luck, and remember, a faculty room can be a calm respite or a side quest of stress.

Activity Putting Tip #45 Into Action: Working Relationships

Directions: Create a list of people you can work with. Share your thoughts with your PLN with the hashtag **#50TeacherTipsBook**.

Tip 46: Differentiating Instruction by Providing Station Rotation and Scaffolded Student Choice

Differentiating instruction is one of the most challenging forms of instruction to implement in our classrooms. Our goal as educators is to meet every learner where they are, so our lessons must be strategic in providing many different avenues for students to take on their learning journeys. Luckily, one instructional model and a strategy can allow us to differentiate instruction effectively. The instructional model is Station Rotation, and the strategy is Scaffold Student Choice. Combined, it creates an effective model to provide many learning opportunities for our students to bridge learning gaps while following the curriculum and standards. You can do this regardless of grade and content. It will take building routines and structure over time. But, once they have become ingrained into your classroom, you can teach any content or skill with this model and differentiate for your students in an effective manner.

Differentiating in Modern Classrooms

What does differentiation look like in our classroom? It doesn't necessarily mean personalized learning. Instead, it provides various modalities during a lesson to meet your student's learning needs. Additionally, when considering various modalities and strategies in your lesson, we must consider our students' accommodations in their 504 and Individualized Education Plans (IEPs). We can begin designing our lessons with differentiation in mind.

Station Rotation

Station rotation can be utilized in-person and online for any lesson. Stations can include:

- independent practice
- collaborative work
- adaptive lessons
- student choice
- teacher-led stations.

These stations can be set up across a physical classroom, breakout rooms online, or asynchronous lesson sequences found on a learning management system.

You must develop routines for each type of station you create and the transitions between them. A countdown clock and music can help with transitions between stations. Additionally, the expectations for each type of station you would like your students to participate in must be clear and practiced for them to become second nature. For example, for an adaptive learning station using a tool like iReady, students need to be able to find their device, log in, and begin the lesson or practice provided by them. As a teacher, you must determine how you monitor your students. If you are using devices for many of your stations, having the software to view your student's screens, control where they can go on their computers, and provide feedback is vital, whether in-person or online. Also, when physically present, you must develop routines to move around the room and check in with each group. You can distribute this monitoring if you have additional help or a co-teacher.

Station Rotation and Scaffolded Student Choice

Beginning lessons with a formative assessment provides guided practice and gradual release. Once that has occurred, several stations may be formed that work on various skills that the lesson requires the students to practice. These stations include the content learned for that specific lesson, a station dedicated to small group instruction with the teacher, and a station dedicated to a student choice board that includes opportunities for Makerspace, coding, or additional practice related to the content discussed. The last station is dedicated to using an adaptive EdTech tool for further practice and refinement. Overall, each station can be done in any order since the formative assessment and guided practice has already been completed. Each station can last ten to twenty minutes.

Additionally, the number of stations can decrease for shorter lessons and class periods. It depends on the scope of the lesson and time.

How is this scaffolding student choice? Ultimately, one station in the example provided is student choice-oriented. Also, a formative assessment and guided practice already took place before the stations, which set up the guided instruction before the stations were introduced. This sets up the scaffolds to give students a foundation on the concepts provided before the stations commence and the student choice-oriented station.

Conclusion - Station Rotation and Scaffolded Student Choice Make Differentiation Possible

Incorporating station rotation as one of your main instructional models and developing the routines to implement it quickly provides opportunities to teach students through multiple modalities. Additionally, it allows teachers to deploy scaffolded student choice within a station to provide them with various avenues they can use in their learning. Whether it is refinement or extension, the stations and the student choice make that possible. Also, within classrooms without boundaries, station rotation and scaffolded student choice can occur virtually and online, depending on whether the station is dedicated in-person or online. Therefore, the choices are endless, and the opportunities to support all of our learners through differentiating instruction.

Activity Putting Tip #46 Into Action: Planning Station Rotation

Directions: Create a lesson plan for implementing station rotation in your class for an upcoming lesson. Start with three to four stations and discuss how they will work to meet your lesson objective. Share your thoughts with your PLN with the hashtag **#50TeacherTipsBook**.

Lesson Objective:			
Whole Group Instruction:			
Station 1	Station 2	Station 3	Station 4 (Optional)
Reflection or Assessment/Exit Ticket:			

Tip 47: Your Experiences Are the Baseline. Their Experience Counts More.

In teaching, building relationships with your class is essential. But for rigor, relevance, and relationships (the three "Rs"), Casey shares that the most critical "R" is relevance. In his two books (Jakubowski, 2020 & Jakubowski, 2021), he noted how relevance helps students understand how the content you are teaching applies to their life and LIVED experience. For a number of our students, the lived experiences of urban and rural students differ from the experiences of most teachers within the profession (suburban). You teach what you know and find out if you don't know.

You can use daily life to talk with students about a wide range of information. Student activities, sports, personal lives, and interests all have applications to the content you are teaching, and they are learning. Your goal is to help students who have never experienced learning about a topic gain the ability to learn from "near" experiences. Called the Zone of Proximal Development or ZPD by a famous Russian psychologist, the theory indicates that students who learn a topic too familiar are bored. If the students learn a topic too far away, they become frustrated or shut down (Shabini, et al., 2010). As a teacher, you need to see how well students work on new concepts that relate to, spiraled, or scaffolded from previously learned materials. When you are in the Zone, your students learn how to learn, especially by cognitively modeling how a learner attacks a problem from the do know, researches what they do not know, and combines the two into new knowledge.

Also, remember that learning is very different for every student. How you teach a concept may work for you, but you might miss the learning for the student, and at the end of the day, the whole educational operation is really about student learning. With students accessing technology, we assume that basics such as how to look up information or what constitutes research are taught. That line of thinking is flawed. Start thinking with KWL charts, what you know, want to know, and have learned about subjects. Ask students to self-rate or describe their comfort level. When teaching about fractions, use pizza or cake. Bring in experiences that will help students concretely with their thinking about a subject. Focus on the emotions students are displaying as you move into subjects.

When creating a community of learners, be aware of placing children on the spot in class. Try using various question and answer techniques to help students address their thought process instead of just the correct answer. Pay attention to gender issues, as the developmental process for boys and girls differs by age. Also, closely watch cultural differences, as some children in different ethnic communities will not look a figure of authority in the eyes. It is disrespectful. Be aware of how different the United States school system is today than ten years ago. Not just COVID-19, but a wide range of incidents has changed the demographics of our nation and introduced new diversity and opportunities.

As we adjust to new normals, be aware of how different some children have experienced schooling across the United States. Some children have arrived at your school missing significant years. We have lost camp experiences, gained virtual schooling, and witnessed different parts of the United States experience different narratives about several historical and current events.

Our students will need help with language acquisition as our nation gains more individuals who have started life elsewhere. This includes parents, who will seek ways to support their children while they learn the structures of American life, and the idioms of English in the states. Patience will become more than a virtue. It will become a necessity. Focus on strengths-based education- and always remain positive. Each student is a work of art in progress.

Activity Putting Tip #47 Into Action: Strengths in our student's

Directions: Use the strengths that your students bring to the classroom. How can you shine a light on their strengths? Share your thoughts with your PLN with the hashtag **#50TeacherTipsBook**.

I Know	They Know	Connections

Tip 48: Teacher Reflections and Self-Evaluations

Congratulations! You have made it to the end of the school year. Your students have gone through an incredible learning experience. Each obstacle was hurdled with grace (or as much gracefulness as you could muster), and the year is wrapping up. You've guided your students through empowering reflections and helped them conceptualize the school year and the person they have become through it. There is one last step for you to complete.

It is time for your self-reflection and evaluation. No, we are not discussing your end-of-year teacher evaluations (mine were often not completed until well into the following year, as standardized test scores counted for most of our evaluation). This is your space. Each year should end with personal reflection and an evaluation of your process. It is guided and driven by you to create an environment of growth within your profession.

Similar to guiding student reflections, it is crucial to guide your self-reflections with purpose. Before you dig into your evaluation, consider this: What do you want to get out of your reflections? Bearing that question in mind, craft your reflections in a way that aids your goals. If you wish to gain confidence, grow your skills and abilities as a teacher, and prepare yourself for improvement, your self-evaluation should be geared towards those elements.

You may realize just how much there is to reflect on at year-end. So much happens in any given week of teaching, let alone an entire school year. Therefore, it is a good idea to take your time and focus on the entire body of work for the year. Check this bullet point list to help you reflect on some critical regions of your pedagogy. It is not exhaustive, and you may want to add to it. Remember, this is for your growth and improvement, not for beating yourself up, harping on mistakes, or stressing yourself out over things outside your control.

- **Classroom Environment -** Was your classroom warm and welcoming to students? Did it encourage or hinder productivity? What would you keep from how you arranged your classroom? What would you like to add? What feedback did students give you about their learning space? Are there issues that need to be brought up to your school leaders / custodial crew to keep the classroom in good repair?
- **Student Relationships -** What percentage of students did you feel confident in identifying their strengths/weaknesses in academics? Outside of academics? What opportunities did you provide to meet with students individually? In groups? How did students express concerns/needs/suggestions? How can you improve on relationships next year?
- **Self-Care -** What did you do well regarding work/life balance? How would you rate your nutrition, exercise, and sleep routines? What small changes would you like to implement next year to maintain your health and high energy levels?
- **Pedagogy -** What were your best pedagogical strategies this year? Did you find yourself relying on a specific strategy more than others? Have you been introduced to any new strategies you would like to implement or learn more about? Where can you find more information about that skill?
- **Teacher Relationships -** What educators did you learn from this year? Who can you rely on for advice (you can also break this down into specific areas, i.e., subject area, classroom management, etc.)? Do you have a professional learning community inside your school? Outside of it? Online (Twitter, Facebook groups, etc.)?
- **Confidence check -** What did you do well? How did you feel you impacted your students? What lessons/lesson plan ideas did you come up with that were more engaging than expected? What made you feel a strong sense of self-efficacy in the classroom?

This list is a starting point, but please continue to reflect on your year with every piece of relevant information you can find. Focus on your strengths and continue building on them. Each year can be better than the last. I believe in you and hope you are developing an empowering belief in yourself.

Activity Putting Tip #48 Into Action: Self-Reflect and Evaluate

Directions: Self-reflect and evaluate the following areas this tip discusses. How are you doing in these areas during or at the end of the school year? Share your thoughts with your PLN with the hashtag **#50TeacherTipsBook**.

Classroom Environment	
Student Relationships	
Self-Care	
Pedagogy	
Teacher Relationships	
Self-Confidence	

Tip 49: Digital Classroom Norms and Routines Are Also Classroom Management

We must develop routines and norms around student device management, including logging into and navigating applications and EdTech tools. Without direction and consistent reinforcement, precious minutes of class will be taken to complete these tasks. Ultimately, we want these tasks to be automatic as our students must also navigate digital classroom spaces that require a whole set of norms and routines like in our physical classroom spaces. Similar to those physical classroom routines, modeling, clarity, repetition, and thinking less is more can be linked to developing good habits and routines for your students while completing digital activities. Additionally, we will touch on digital citizenship and cell phone norms.

Modeling

First, we must begin with modeling. We must model how to turn on the device. Enter the username and password credentials. Be sure to have your students' usernames and passwords available in case a student forgets their credentials. We must model how to navigate various applications and how they work. For example, model how students can navigate your learning management system (LMS) - where they can access assignments and create content to demonstrate their learning and how they can communicate with you, the teacher, in that digital space. After the initial modeling is provided over the first week or two using that digital tool, create a series of screencasts and place them on your LMS so students can always access them if they forget how to access and navigate a tool you are using in class.

Teacher Clarity

Second, we need to focus on being transparent in our modeling and how we provide directions. This is teacher clarity. It is best to model in manageable chunks that are scaffolded over time. For example, when using a digital tool at first, the beginning tasks will be less complex and easier to complete. The task can become more complex as more experience with the tool is gained. While using a tool such as Google Slides, the first task may involve students completing one slide in a collaborative activity. In contrast, the more complex task done later on involves them completing an entire presentation, including graphics or notes.

Thinking Less is More

Third, repetition is vital while thinking less is more. Choose 3-5 digital tools and use them consistently for various classroom tasks so students can practice regularly. Through this consistency students' routines and habits will become ingrained.

Digital Citizen and Cell Phones

Classroom management also involves modeling what citizenship looks like in both the physical and the digital realms. We must demonstrate the appropriate uses of a digital tool for educational purposes versus personal and entertainment purposes. Additionally, as we would in a physical space, we must redirect students if they are off-task. We must know what students are doing, whether that monitoring takes place through software or simply walking around the classroom. Cell phone policy varies widely across schools. Like any tool, teachers can incorporate cell phones into classroom instruction if policy allows. First, determine the school's policies regarding cell phone use. Then, develop routines and norms around their use in your classroom. Can they be actively used for learning purposes, or can they be placed on desks, or should they be out of sight? Norms should be based on the classroom culture you believe would best benefit your learners and your classroom management preferences.

Managing and navigating classrooms now takes place in multiple realms. We aim to intentionally teach routines over time to establish and maintain a positive classroom culture. As you begin formulating your classroom management plan, think less is more. Start by developing classroom norms and routines. Over the year, review the norms and routines as much as possible. You can add more digital and tech routines but keep them simple. Mentioned last here but not least important, focus on developing relationships with your students. The relationships with your students individually and collectively will make or break your norms and routines regardless of whether your classroom is physical or digital.

Activity Putting Tip #49 Into Action: Develop Your Own Digital Classroom Management Plan

Directions: Develop your own digital classroom management plan. Use strategies from this tip and other tips found in this book to develop this plan. Create a list of routines that you will use to establish and then maintain these norms. Share your thoughts with your PLN with the hashtag **#50TeacherTipsBook**.

Digital Classroom Routines
How Will You Establish and Maintain These Routines?

Tip 50: Knowing When to Retreat

Not all first-time teaching jobs will be your fairy tale. Our careers have been a journey through different jobs, but one entire career for many of us. In college, we are subjected to the ideal narrative, the best scenario, the perfection of the position, the career, the vocation. But the reality is not always like the textbooks (see tip 38 on theory versus practice). We are here to tell you:

IT IS OKAY. YOU CAN FEEL YOUR FEELINGS.

If you start to feel a burning sensation in your head, heart, or gut, it's okay to start looking for a new place to practice your craft. If a sports star can request a trade, you can look elsewhere to apply your craft. Why would you do this? There are several different reasons. First, the grade level may not be a great fit. Remember, you have all of grades K-6 or grades 7-12 in your subject area to explore. Sometimes the differences in maturity levels among students vary so dramatically over the six years that grade 7 in middle school can be a different level than grade 12.

Second, in larger schools, your team may not be a great fit. You may work with several colleagues, some of whom disagree with you and your philosophy. You need to know that after self-reflection, you may need to move to a different team to survive, let alone thrive. If you are constantly self-doubting, I suggest looking for a different team. You may have run into experiential learning- meaning conflict.

Third, you are in a school district or community, not where you pictured yourself taking the career path. It happens to the best of us, as we are swept up in the agony of needing that FIRST JOB when we need to look at the best fit for our careers. Casey has experienced this and learned that the first job is not always the best. Take it slowly and ask probing questions about the new school's culture. You have a framework of like-minded teachers who can help one grow in a way that is aligned with their mission and interests.

Fourth, family. This is a big reason people need to move. You may have left your family "back home," and the time you spent was a little too lonely. Or you found that special someone and you two want to hit the road, relocate, or find a place closer or matches your vision for a couple of people who are starting a life together.

Fifth- money. Sigh, because it often happens. There is a loyalty penalty in many fields, where staying with one employer for too long can make a severe dent in your future earnings. Teaching pay scales are often very different in areas across the United States, and especially at the middle and upper ends, different places in the same county can have up to 10,000 dollars difference in salary, benefits, and earning opportunities. Never be beholden to a location indebted to you. Your best bet is to create a list of the following:

Figure 50.1

Cost-Benefit Analysis of Teaching Job Prospect

Pay	Benefits	Commute Time	Geography	Community Resources/ Activities

Once you figure out what is your best bet, go for it. Also, don't forget that education careers are more than just classroom teaching. You can leave the classroom and become a professional developer. Or you can go into administration. You can serve as an expert for a company on training and material for professional activities. You can always get a degree in a new field. Remember, a career is not a sentence to a hard time, it is a journey.

Activity Putting Tip #50 Into Action: Breaking Down Your Skillset

Directions: After completing the cost-benefit analysis above for a teaching position, create a list of the skills you've developed and built as a teacher. Write them down, and then think about their appearance in a different position. Share your thoughts with your PLN with the hashtag **#50TeacherTipsBook**.

My Skills in Teaching Are:

What Do They Look Like in a Different Job?

Critical Conversation Four: Shifting and Toggling Through Multiple Learning Environments

Though no one has all the answers to any situation, we can learn from the mistakes and successes during the past few years of teaching through a pandemic. After all, there never was a course during college titled "Pandemic Teaching 101." COVID-19 thrust educators into a world of teaching online and hybrid learning experiences. We were learning alongside our students what it was like to teach and learn in this new space. With COVID-19 cases decreasing (at the time of this writing), we can reflect on best practices during this uncertain time of teaching to help us design classrooms that move between in-person and online, which we believe will be a mainstay moving forward into the future.

Sam: As spaces look different, so are the teaching practices, so let's talk about some basics. Before we jump into strategies and best practices, what terminology do we need to familiarize our readers with?

Matt: I believe that when we're talking about navigating these classroom spaces, strategies can work across various settings. However, they may appear different. Before we jump into specific strategies, you must understand that we need infrastructure to teach within any of these settings. For example, the first thing we truly need is a learning management system (LMS). We need an LMS because it can be transferable to any teaching setting. We can deliver our assignments and tasks and communicate with students. I like to use the airport analogy, using the LMS as an airport to various other avenues and tools you want to use. Use tools like Zoom, Google Meets, or Microsoft Teams for synchronous sessions, depending on your district. Specific engagement style tools are based on your district. Still, you'll usually have engagement, assessment, and collaboration tools.

Kevin: The next step is to consider synchronous versus asynchronous. Different learning management systems play better towards different learning styles when synchronously or asynchronously. For example, learning is at your own pace, depending on your district and what's happening within that district and your communities. There may be times when you are required or possibly have the option of being synchronous or asynchronous. You can decide if I want to meet my students at the same time, in the same space online, or if I want to provide some program where they can respond at their own pace. It's essential to consider what is your learning management system and what's going to play better into that, and also, just as importantly, actually, more importantly, what are your community needs. To be clear, the school district selects the LMS. You, the teacher, can select the EdTech tools you use in your classroom. In addition, teachers can often choose what lessons are asynchronous or synchronous.

For example, when the pandemic started, I was in a very low-income community with a considerable lack of technology. With no face-to-face option and minimal technology, the school tried to push a lot of synchronous activities and what we noticed was attendance would be around three or so. It wasn't convenient for that situation, so we, as teachers, ended up providing many asynchronous tools and programs that students could get into at their own pace.

That was crucial for the community at the start of the pandemic, after grant funding and programs where students were provided with laptops and WiFi. Synchronous activities became much more widespread in that district because there was more access and availability. However, some of my students at the high school level were still working during the day, watching kids, helping siblings, helping their parents, whatever the case might be. We must first ask what the community needs, what resources we have available, and how we can match those things.

Casey: The first point I want to raise is that we sometimes don't even have Internet or bandwidth as rural educators and learners. We need to be aware that they may have the technology tools of the phone, the iPad, or the Chromebook. But they may not have the ability to get on the information highway. Second of all, what we also need to be well and truly aware of is the assumptions we make about digital natives versus digital visitors.

Avoid making assumptions that our students know how to do certain operations we take for granted. I think our best practice is to begin at the beginning, assuming that nobody knows how to do anything.

Sam: Let's jump into techniques and strategies and share some of the best practices we learned through COVID-19. Which tools did you bring back into the face-to-face classroom?

Matt: I love the strategy Think, Pair, Share. This activity can be incorporated into Google Slides, Jamboard, or any slideshow or interactive slide deck. First, provide a prompt or problem for students to solve individually, responding if their slide deck is interactive (Nearpod, Peardeck, or Lumio). Then allow them to pair in small breakout rooms or in person. After they've responded, they can further discuss or evaluate what they've done and share it with the rest of the class.

As the teacher, you see all students' responses on their slides. You can provide covert feedback to them if you would like.

Kevin: One of my favorite things before the pandemic was a student choice assignment. We would discuss what it looks like when that concept is mastered as a class. Students got the option of figuring out how to bridge that gap by learning about it, demonstrating it, and showing mastery of it.

I felt that that played a fantastic role in an online setting because many of my students had varying degrees of knowledge of technology and comfort levels. When I gave them student choice options, it was really about developing rubrics or developing some method they understand very clearly. Then it's up to them to figure out how they want to do that demonstration. Flexibility became very important. All students still showed me that they knew the content. We were confident with their learning and were beginning to master those concepts.

Giving students flexibility and allowing them to choose how they show their knowledge is an excellent strategy in person but an even more critical strategy online. This experience allowed them to decide on a program they were comfortable with, which would be the carrier to show this knowledge. They didn't have to leave their comfort zone with the technology. Instead, they could focus on the content.

Casey: I don't require my students to have their cameras on. I think that part of it is that we need to treat them as agency-based individuals. Sometimes we don't want our cameras on, or we don't want to expose others to the reality of our lives. We all have our home life, school life, and work life. Another best practice for me is the use of polls. I want to hear from my students. I like quick polls like thumbs up, thumbs down, or ratings on a scale of one to five, so I can get a sense of how they're doing without a big issue.

Sam: What is a piece of advice that you wish you knew before you started into this whole hybrid of virtual things?

Casey: Never trust the technology to work. Even if you've practiced on it, without a doubt, the technology will smell your fear. Always have a backup plan.

Kevin: Students often imitate your commitment to the lesson by your passion for it. It's imperative to think about how they would read your body language if they were live in your class. Present those same things in an online forum as much as possible. A peppy, cheerful voice excites students just from your tonality if it's a synchronous lesson with positive body posture.

If you're even doing something asynchronous, and maybe it's not a video, they can't see you, consider the tone of the texts. While giving directions, you can pepper that with language that excites them about what they will learn. Now, even with that, you may have similar learners who are not super enthusiastic, but you want to set the tone.

Matt: I would say that digital routines are just as important as physical in-person class routines. Regardless of my teaching, I always like to start with a two-week boot camp at the beginning of the semester so students can learn the routines that fall into our digital and physical spaces and how they can come together.

After that two-week boot camp, keep those routines in place, and you and your students will feel more comfortable implementing and using the various types of tools in the classroom. Students need to understand the expectations of in-person and virtual classrooms, what's acceptable versus what's not, and what being a good citizen looks like in both spaces. After setting expectations through the initial onboarding, continue to 'think less is more' not to overwhelm them. Focus on more manageable expectations at first, and build from there.

Final Thoughts - Critical Conversation #4

COVID-19 threw us into a situation for which none of us were prepared. We were required to teach students online with little to no training. We had to scramble to quickly move from a face-to-face learning environment to a remote one. It took a lot to learn how to teach in the online space. With COVID-19 slowly moving behind us, we can now take the time to reflect and breathe. Teaching online has taught us the power of grace over grades and the importance of connecting with students outside of class, and giving myself space to process and work through new tools and strategies.

Teaching is hard - teaching during a pandemic is 100% harder. I believe that we came out more robust, and the experience of teaching online helped equip us for digital learning days with strategies to engage our students. We hope that this Critical Conversation helped to inspire and motivate you to keep going. For more EdTech tips, check out various tips, such as Tip 32.

CONCLUSION – CRUSH IT FROM THE START

You made it. Whether you read this book from start to finish or are picking and choosing which tips, strategies, and Critical Conversations you would like to learn more about, we are honored by the work you are doing to make an impact. Throughout this book, we have discussed many tips and strategies that we hope you can think about, reflect on, and begin thinking about implementing within your teaching practice.

Additionally, our hope through the Critical Conversations is to prepare you to navigate challenging issues and problems teachers and schools have to experience in our current educational climate. We chose these Critical Conversation topics because we felt they would be ongoing challenges teachers must navigate. As with any significant challenge within education, we expect further evolution and growth, and we intend to hope you can take your experiences and research to bolster your toolkit in navigating these difficult conversations and experiences teachers have to experience in our schools.

Moving Forward Into Further Growth

After finishing reading this for the first time, we hope you will continue to come back to this book. The ultimate goal is to have it be a continuous resource and an opportunity for you to connect with a greater community of teachers worldwide to support one another. Education, specifically teaching, is highly challenging. Yet, we want our work together to make it easier for you to navigate and enjoy it to the highest possible level sustainably. In addition to you and your students, your family, friends, and professional learning network will benefit from this because the effects are exponential. Last, we hope learning these various tips and strategies has been inspiring and has fired you up as a teacher.

How to Connect With Each Other - Teachers Connecting is #BetterTogether

We want to reiterate how important it is for all of us to connect and continue to support each other into the future. Using the hashtag **#50TeacherTipsBook**, we can all work together to amplify how we teach and navigate education as it is ever-changing in a world that is changing faster than we can blink. To move forward sustainably in education, we must work together collectively. As you know, locally and globally, there are many problems that we must tackle in education. Individually, we cannot solve them. However, collectively, we can. On an individual level, having a group of dedicated teachers supporting each other is powerful. You can access resources and support beyond the book by contacting teachers locally and globally.

How to Connect With Us

To connect with the four authors of this book, follow them on Twitter and use the hashtag **#50TeacherTipsBook**. We would also enjoy hearing your teacher tips and strategies and may feature them in an upcoming blog or future edition of this book. Ultimately, we want to provide teachers with the opportunity to share their knowledge and wisdom in navigating this ever-changing profession. Therefore, we have included a QR Code below and a bit.ly link to a Google Form to collect your responses.

https://bit.ly/tipsform

Extending Your Learning

Beyond this book, we hope you extend your learning by connecting with educators and taking advantage of the great resources for teachers. Opportunities exist, such as building your professional learning network, reading and listening to education and teaching-themed blogs and podcasts, and joining and participating in professional associations.

Build Your Professional Learning Network

Previously, you had members of your college class help you with group projects. Now, as a novice teacher, your school colleagues will become the start of your Professional Learning Network. Yet, the four of us will share that the advent of the internet, including social media, like Twitter, has expanded our Professional contacts far beyond geography, and now we work with people very far beyond our locality. You can find great people on the internet in professional organizations and interest groups who can help and support you. We highly recommend you find one hour a month to engage in what is referred to as "chats" on Twitter, Facebook Live, or Instagram. You can have professional development during chats or "live" events, engage in collegial conversations, and ask for help and resources. Here are some (as of 2022) hashtags to follow for PLNs.

- #sschat for social studies
- #crazypln for all education-related topics
- #edtech for all education technology related
- #iteachmath, #mathchat, and #mtbos for all math-related education topics
- #engchat for all English-related education topics
- #scichat for all science-related education topics
- #elemchat for all related elementary education-related topics
- #mschat for all middle school related education topics
- #mfltwitterati for all foreign language and English as a Second Language education-related topics
- #edchat for all topics related to talking about education
- #stem for all science, technology, engineering, and mathematic education topics
- #edleadership for all education leadership-related education topics
- #teachertwitter for all teaching and education related topics

Follow Education Blogs and Podcasts

Teaching and education blogs and podcasts are a great way to learn about practical strategies, experiences, and ideas you can think about possibly implementing in your classroom. Across the world, teachers, researchers, and educational leaders are taking their expertise and creating these learning opportunities (many of which are free). We recommend subscribing to several blogs and podcasts to read during a break in planning or providing student feedback and to listen to while you commute to and from your school. You will encounter every topic imaginable to learn more about from instruction, EdTech, culturally responsive teaching, social-emotional learning, and more.

Join Professional Organizations

Another way to continue your growth as an educator is by joining professional organizations. Professional organizations give you opportunities to attend conferences and access journals and webinars. Some professional organizations are free, while others have associated costs. Consider joining a professional organization to support learning in your field. You can search for professional organizations related to your specific concentration area. Below are a few that we recommend:

- National Educator Association - https://www.nea.org/
- Council for Exceptional Children - https://exceptionalchildren.org/
- PDK - https://pdkintl.org/
- International Society of Technology Education - https://www.iste.org/
- Association for the Advancement of Computing in Education - https://www.aace.org/
- Association of American Educators - https://www.aaeteachers.org/
- American Educational Research Association - https://www.aera.net/
- American Federation of Teachers https://www.aft.org/
- Kappa Delta Pi - https://www.kdp.org/home
- CUE - https://cue.org/
- National Association for Gifted Children - https://www.nagc.org/

For even more associations, check out these lists: https://districtadministration.com/professional-organizations-for-teachers-and-k-12-leaders/ and https://jobstars.com/education-professional-associations-organizations/.

Teachers Make an Impact

Every day you are making an impact. Never forget that, even when you have the most challenging days. Also, know that your impact on the students and community you serve may not be seen that day or during the school year. We must think of teaching as the ultimate investment. Like our retirement savings, the fruition of that impact may not come to light for many years. Additionally, we must consider that impact on a student as an exponential curve as further learning and experiences accumulate on top of that foundation you have helped build.

Therefore, we must always know that we are making an impact as teachers. While we may see some elements of impact during a school day and school year, we must never forget that our impact is lifelong, and the manifestation transpires after our experience serving that student is over.

Take Care of Yourself - Remember You Are a Business of One

A startling statistic - approximately 40% of new teachers will leave by year five. Teacher burnout, pre-pandemic, was a cause of a rise in recruitment issues in many challenging to staff schools (e.g., urban, suburban, and rural). Some areas, like Special Education, New English Learners, science, math, and technology, faced hiring gaps between the number of openings and the number of people with certifications. Entire states actively poach teachers from other states, offering sign-on bonuses, housing allowances, and other perks, such as a free master's degree or student loan forgiveness. Research and find the best opportunities to support your growth as an educator now and in the future. Here are some tips to take care of yourself:

- Be patient with yourself. Mistakes happen. Please do not harshly critique yourself. You are learning, growing, and evolving what the four of us did in year one versus now (shudder).
- Learn to honor your voice. Ask if you feel something is wrong or skewed. No harm, no foul. In decades, your fresh eyes may be the first new view of a situation.
- It is perfectly okay to say, "I don't know- let's find out together."
- You cannot earn an income if you are sick physically, emotionally, mentally, or spiritually. Take care of yourself via good habits.

The author of *U R A Brand* (Kaputa, 2006) discusses how you are a brand - like any other product. Your knowledge, insights, and ideas are your calling card. Own it, love it, and be aware of social media.

Final Thoughts – Crush it from the Start

We hope you enjoyed reading the **#50TeacherTipsBook** as we pour our experiences, research, and voices into it with the hope of helping you navigate the present and future of education. Teaching is hard work but one of the most fulfilling experiences. We hope that the tips and Critical Conversations can help make teaching and leading students in our ever-changing world more accessible and sustainable.

There will be fulfilling and challenging days. You will feel every emotion: the good, the bad, and the ugly. We've been there, as have your colleagues. We understand.

Most importantly, we believe in you and your local and global connections with teachers also believe in you. Together, we support one another as a community of educators. By being #BetterTogether, we will create the best classrooms we can for our students. We got this! Crush it from the Start!

REFERENCES

Cross, T. L. (1989). *Towards a culturally competent system of care: A monograph on effective services for minority children who are severely emotionally disturbed.* Washington, D.C.: Georgetown Center.

Cisco, K. (2021). Five things educators can do in the middle of a CRT controversy. *Edallies blog.* Downloaded: https://edalliesmn.org/blog/5-things-educators-can-do-in-the-middle-of-a-crt-controversy/

Mathematics Standards. (n.d.). Common Core State Standards Initiative. http://www.corestandards.org/Math/

Cuban, L. (2013). *Inside the black box of classroom practice: Change without reform in American education.* Harvard Education Press.

Donnor, J. K. (2021). White fear, White flight, the rules of racial standing and whiteness as property: Why two critical race theory constructs are better than one. *Educational Policy, 35*(2), 259-273.

Fecich, S. (2018). Edumagic: A guide for Pre-service Teachers. EduMatch.

Fecich, S., Gibson, K, Sansom, H., & Turk, H. (2019). Edumagic Shine On: A guide for New Teachers. EduMatch.

Freire, P. (2000). Pedagogy of the oppressed (30th anniversary ed.). Continuum.

Freudenberger, H. J. (1974). Staff burn-out. *Journal of social issues, 30*(1), 159-165.

Gay, G. (2002). Preparing for culturally responsive teaching. *Journal of teacher education, 53*(2), 106-116.

Goldberg, M. (2021). A frenzy of book banning. *New York Times.* Downloaded: https://www.nytimes.com/2021/11/12/opinion/book-bans.html

Hustad, M. (2014). The brilliance of asking incredibly naive questions. *Fortune.* downloaded from https://fortune.com/2014/02/10/the-brilliance-of-asking-incredibly-naive-questions/

Ingersoll, R., & Kralik, J. M. (2004). The impact of mentoring on teacher retention: What the research says.

Jakubowski, C. (2020). Thinking About Teaching. Alexandra, VA: Edumatch.

Jakubowski, C. (2021). A Cog in the Machine. Alexandra, VA: Edumatch.

Leahy, W., & Sweller, J. (2008). The imagination effect increases with an increased intrinsic cognitive load. *Applied Cognitive Psychology: The Official Journal of the Society for Applied Research in Memory and Cognition, 22*(2), 273-283.

Leichtman, K. (2019). Burnout: The Devastating Impact on a New Teacher. (Publication No. 27664100) [Doctoral Dissertation, Florida Atlantic University]. Proquest Dissertations and Theses Database.Manolev, J., Sullivan, A., & Slee, R. (2019). The datafication of discipline: ClassDojo, surveillance and a performative classroom culture. *Learning, Media and Technology, 44*(1), 36-51.

McGarr, O. (2021). The use of virtual simulations in teacher education to develop pre-service teachers' behavior and classroom management skills: implications for reflective practice. *Journal of Education for Teaching, 47*(2), 274-286.

McKinney, G., Rondot, Z. (2021). The Expert Effect. Alexandra, VA: Edumatch

Merga, M. K. (2020). School librarians as literacy educators within a complex role. *Journal of Library Administration,* 60(8), 889-908.

Milner, H. R., Harmon, M. D., & McGee, E. (2021). Critical Race Theory, Teacher Education, and the "New" Focus on Racial Justice. In *Handbook of Critical Race Theory in Education* (pp. 364-378). Routledge.

Misco, T., & Patterson, N. C. (2007). A study of pre-service teachers' conceptualizations of academic freedom and controversial issues. *Theory & Research in Social Education, 35*(4), 520-550.

Miller, K. E. (2021). A Light in Students' Lives: K-12 Teachers' Experiences (Re) Building Caring Relationships during Remote Learning. *Online learning, 25(1), 115-134.*

Moses, E. (2021). My Name is an address. Alexandria, VA: Edumatch Publishing.

National Center for Education Statistics. (2022). Students With Disabilities. Condition of Education. U.S. Department of Education, Institute of Education Sciences. Retrieved June 2nd, 2022, from https://nces.ed.gov/programs/coe/indicator/cgg.

Ravitch, D. (2016). The death and life of the great American school system: How testing and choice are undermining education. Basic Books.

Redding, C., & Nguyen, T. D. (2020). Recent trends in the characteristics of new teachers, the schools in which they teach, and their turnover rates. *Teacher College Record, 122* (7), 1-36.

Rowling, J. K. (2014). Harry Potter and the Prisoner of Azkaban. Bloomsbury Children's Books.

Rumberger, A. (2019). The elementary school library: Tensions between access and censorship. *Contemporary Issues in Early Childhood, 20*(4), 409-421.

Schafer, K. (2021). America's Public School Teachers are far less diverse than their students. *Pew Research.* Downloaded: https://www.pewresearch.org/fact-tank/2021/12/10/americas-public-school-teachers-are-far-less-racially-and-ethnically-diverse-than-their-students/

Scribner, C. F. (2016). *The fight for local control.* Cornell University Press.

Seleznyov, S., Goei, S. L., & Ehren, M. (2021). International policy borrowing and the case of Japanese Lesson Study: culture and its impact on implementation and adaptation. *Professional Development in Education*, 1-15.

Shabani, K., Khatib, M., & Ebadi, S. (2010). Vygotsky's zone of proximal development: Instructional implications and teachers' professional development. *English language teaching,* 3(4), 237-248.

Staff, W. (2021). What Teachers Need to Know About Restorative Justice. Retrieved 14 June 2022, from https://www.weareteachers.com/restorative-justice/

Sweller, J. (1988). Cognitive load during problem solving: Effects on learning. *Cognitive Science*, 12, 257–285. https://doi.org/10.1207/s15516709cog1202_4

Washor, E., & Mojkowski C. (2014). Student disengagement: It's deeper than you think. *Phi Delta Kappan, 95*(8), 8-

LIST OF FIGURES

ABOUT THE AUTHORS

Matthew Rhoads, Ed.D., is an expert and innovator in educational technology and instructional strategy integration within online, blended, and traditional in-person classroom settings. As a practicing technology leader, trainer, integrationist, and coach in Adult Education, K-12, and Higher Education, he develops EdTech tool integrations with research-based instructional strategies to drive instruction. He also has expertise in instructing teachers and educational leaders on how to utilize data to make data-driven decisions to drive instruction as well as has developed a data literacy curriculum for K-20 educators. Dr. Rhoads publications focus on integrating instructional strategies with EdTech tools to amplify student learning within in-person, online, and blended learning classrooms. His latest books include *Instruction Without Boundaries: Enhance Your Teaching Strategies with Technology Tools in Any Setting, Amplify Learning: A Global Collaborative - Amplifying Instructional Design*, and *Navigating the Toggled Term: A Guide for K-12 Classroom and School Leaders*. He also has his podcast, Navigating Education - The Podcast, which discusses all topics related to education and instruction. For more information on Dr. Rhoads and his work, visit his website at www.matthewrhoads.com.

Casey Jakubowski, Ph.D., is a recognized expert and consultant in leadership, social studies instruction and curriculum integration. Dr. J focuses on civics education, rural education, and teacher mentoring and educational administration development. After 20 plus years in the classroom, and as an administrator and State Education Department school improvement and curriculum specialist in New York State, Dr J. works with Education Doctoral candidates at a research university in Maryland. Jakubowski has published extensively on rural education, and has three books, including *Thinking About Teaching, A Cog in the Machine*, and *Getting to the HEARTS of Teaching: Humanities, education, arts, technology and science for a collaborative classroom*. Casey is active on twitter : @caseyj_edu and has a blog: https://ctjakubowski.weebly.com/.

Samantha (Sam) Fecich earned her Ph.D. in learning, design, and technology from Penn State University. In addition, she has an M.Ed. in special education and one in instructional technology, both from Penn State. Her PA certifications include K-12 special education, K-12 elementary education, and Pre-K to sixth-grade teaching. Dr. Fecich has taught education for eight years at a small liberal arts college in Pennsylvania. She is the author of "*EduMagic: A Guide for Preservice Teachers*" and "*EduMagic Shine On A Guide for New Teachers*." Dr. Fecich also hosts the EduMagic Podcast for future teachers. Dr. Sam loves a good PSL (pumpkin space latte) and taking walks with her family. You can find her on Twitter and Instagram @SFecich. Check out her work at www.SFecich.com.

Kevin Leichtman earned his Ph.D and Master's degree from Florida Atlantic University, where he also serves as an adjunct professor teaching equity and diversity courses to pre-service educators. He taught ELA, Reading, and ESOL in each grade from 7-12 over the span of 8 years. He has authored two books, *Teacher's Guide to the Mental Edge* and *The Perfect Ten: Ten Students, Ten Mindsets, One New Definition of Perfection*. Kevin continues his work in education through tlceducate.com , a company that he co-founded alongside his wife, Dr. Anala Leichtman. They met, got married, and had their first child all while pursuing their doctorates in the same program.

Made in United States
North Haven, CT
01 February 2023

31964499R00091